MEN'S RULES

HOW TO MEET A GIRL
AND
A GUIDE TO HEALTHY RELATIONSHIPS

CONTENTS

INTRODUCTION

If you're reading this book, then you've found what you were looking for.

Who is this book for? For everyone who is ready to change his life for the better and become a happier person. No matter how old you are, it's never too late to become a happy man. To do that, you need to challenge yourself. Once you start reading this book, you're halfway to figuring out exactly what kind of girl you want.

You'll learn about basic rules, beliefs, and principles that will allow you to make your own life happy and effective when it comes to women. The book will help to shape and improve your model of seduction and communication with women.

A huge number of men are asking questions: How to meet a girl? What to talk about with a girl? How do you know a girl likes you? How do you make a girl chase you? How to tell a girl you love her? And so on. This book is designed to give answers to all these questions. You'll be able to figure out exactly what you need to do so you don't have to ask these questions anymore.

You may have various goals. Maybe you want to find out how to easily seduce and have sex with a girl on the first day. Or how to find the one girl you can spend the rest of your life with. If you're already dating a girl, and you're having relationship problems, you'll be able to figure out how to solve them or make a decision to end this relationship. This book will help you in all cases.

Before you start seducing or looking for that one girl, you need to start with yourself. I realize it's corny, and you've probably read a bunch of self-development books. But without self-development, you can't get ahead even in the easiest moments in dating and relationships with girls. Everything is interconnected. That's why the first part is called – "Men's Rules". Here you'll understand where to start in order to become the kind of guy that girls will want and respect.

There are no super formulas or cool dialogues. Everything is described here in simple terms, briefly and clearly. Examples and short stories from life will help you understand the essence of what's written so that you don't repeat the same mistakes.

CHAPTER 1: MEN'S RULES

I Want, I Do, I Get

Guys have a lot of problems that are similar to each other, and these problems are basic. That is, they seem to be very simple, but at the same time, they are absolutely not obvious to many guys. That's why I decided to write a series of sections dedicated just to those basic rules, basic principles, and basic beliefs. Having these beliefs greatly simplifies life and makes it much more effective.

Also, we will talk about how these rules directly affect your communication with the opposite sex. These rules can be projected onto all other aspects of your life as well.

Today we're going to talk about this important rule, "I WANT, I DO, I GET".

First things first. The first word in this rule is "I WANT." What is it about? And how, in fact, to approach it?

First, you have to be clear about what you want. For many, figuring out what we want (as each of us understands what he wants on an intuitive level) is not so easy.

Let's start with a situation and talk about that category of guys who, for example, don't have a particular girlfriend right now. When we talk about what you might want, you have to openly admit to yourself, what do you want? For example, you want to get a girlfriend, so that you can have dating, sex, maybe even a relationship. It's actually not as easy as it sounds.

First of all: a lot of people find it very hard to admit it to themselves. If you admit you want it (and you don't have it at this moment), it means something is not going well, and you've got a problem with it. And admitting to yourself that you have a problem is hard enough. Sometimes, it gets to the point where guys convince themselves that they don't need it. That is, they live in a space and a reality where they don't seem to want it. But what they put into that reality is that they may walk down the street and stare at some girl or come home and watch porn. But admitting that you want that element in your life (meeting girls) and having your life full of that kind of stuff is hard enough.

I want to tell you about a moment that really turned my life upside down. If I'm not mistaken, it was 2004. My friend and I went out to drink beer. We'd go out to crowded places where, among other things, there were girls. And you kind of hope that in all the years that Santa Claus hasn't given you presents, it will somehow happen on its own. That said, no one would admit to wanting to meet a girl. We just were out, like, having a beer. Drinking beer with a friend and talking. A girl came up, a pretty girl. The girl was talking to me (I now understand, probably, why). Because, contrasted with my friend, I was well-dressed and looked more expensive. At that age, I understood that investing a certain amount of money (which I earned at a part-time job) in clothes is a top priority, as it really affects the first impression of you. She turned to me and said; "hey, I can see that you want all the girls in the world to be yours." At that moment, I probably felt the same emotions as you do now. The whole thing was like a kind of plot of a book, where a girl comes up on her own and asks a question like that, which is quite cliché. I was nineteen years old at the time. I read Remarque then, all that kind of romantic shit, mostly. I was like, "No, I don't need all the girls, I only need one like you". In fact, it's even a little embarrassing to remember the nonsense I was saying at that moment.

Then it became known that it had been creative marketing of pickup training. They hired beautiful girls who would walk down the street, meet guys, and urge them to come to events. A guy would go there, and they would offer him the training directly.

I tried to get to know her and get her phone number. In the end, we agreed that if I came to the event, she would meet me for coffee afterwards. I never went to that training. She turned my life upside down, though.

I went to my dorm, we had an internet connection there.

I went to the website that was on the card she gave me, and I began to absorb the information, which was there. There was information about dating, about some inner fears, about the need to accept and understand it all, etc.

The main impetus of this event was that I became interested in the topic of dating. I realized that I want to meet girls, I want to date, I want to choose by myself, I want to communicate with those people who I'm interested in inside and out, etc. It all began to boil inside of me, wanting to burst out. It is necessary to understand and know clearly, why are you doing it? What do you want?

I went to university, where there were a lot of guys. They were attractive and well-built, with a sense of humor, not stupid, and almost no one had a steady girlfriend. Why? Because inside oneself, that desire wasn't triggered; I want it, I want to have it. When you realize what you want, you have to accept that desire, be proud of it, and be able to defend it.

Let's pretend you have a girlfriend. Maybe you met her on the street, on the internet, through acquaintances, it doesn't matter. If you want something with her, that's fine, be proud. You can tell everyone, you don't have to be shy about it. Even if you don't have a girlfriend. You can say, "I WANT dating, I WANT to meet a girl" somewhere at a party with friends. Don't pretend you're not interested, and then immediately drool over the waitress who brings your beer to the table. That's not fair to yourself.

If we're talking directly about a situation where you already have a girlfriend, let's take a simple example. You're on a date, and you're kissing – super. You've moved on to the next stage. And all of a sudden you get a hard-on, and she's like, "Listen, dude, you got a hard-on." You don't have to be embarrassed about it, it's normal. If you want her, it's normal to want a woman. It's normal for sexual desire to arise. You don't have to be afraid of it. You don't have to be ashamed of it. If you want to kiss her, you don't have to be afraid of being caught in that desire. If you want to kiss – be proud. "Yes, I want to kiss." The other question is how effective it is to say directly, "I want to kiss you" and not to do it. You should by no means be ashamed of it.

If you're walking down the street, and you like some girl, and you want to get acquainted with her, you don't have to be ashamed. You don't have to be ashamed, either in front of her or in front of other people around you. You have every right to do it, be proud of this desire, it's absolutely normal for you as a man. Embrace it, you don't have to banish these thoughts. When you're walking down the street, and you see a girl you like, you don't have to look down and be afraid that, God forbid, she'll notice. You should imagine that you are holding a bottle of champagne, and the girls who are walking towards you have glasses in their hands. If you like the girl, pour your attention into her glass. Say to yourself, "I like you." Start with this simple moment. Start living in harmony with your desires, don't be afraid to show them to the girls around you. Don't be afraid to show them to the girls you see.

In a nightclub, that's one of the main weapons. Getting to know each other starts exactly when you show "I like you" with your desire. Start with that, be completely in tune with your desires. Think, what do you want? You have to be clear, what do you want?

You have to do something for the rule "I WANT, I DO, I GET" to work. And men have major problems with that.

There's some girl, and you want to have sex with her, so do something for that. Understand that if you just met her, and you want to go out on a date, then you have to do something to make that happen. Ask her out. If you're on a date, and you're having a normal conversation, then the next thing you have to do (hopefully you want to, and it's consistent with your desires) is kiss her. And once you've kissed, it's totally normal to think about being together with her (on this date or the next) in an intimate setting where it can be more comfortable to communicate. It could be your apartment, your house, your car. For example, you and her may go to some place with a beautiful view and have sex there. But you have to do something.

You may not be able to do it due to a lack of skills, or because she may turn out to be too stupid, but you have to do something for it. And you're the only one responsible for whether you do it or not. You shouldn't expect it to happen by itself. You have to figure out what you want. Ask yourself this question, "What do I have to do to get it?" The answer is very simple. You usually know it yourself, even without any super complicated theories. Start with simple actions. If you succeed, you'll be thinking about something complicated. The responsibility for this is solely yours. That will be nobody's fault but your own if you don't do it. You want to kiss her? Do something for a kiss to happen.

Apply the "Three No's" rule even. Have her stop you three times. If you're sitting with a girl, and you want to kiss her, and you don't do anything to achieve it, don't expect anything good. If you two have already been on a lot of dates, and you want to have sex, but you're not inviting her over, you're not doing anything. How will you get what you want?

"I WANT, I DO, I GET. I WANT and I GET – it won't work that way. This element of DOING, it must be present. If you will be in harmony with your desires, even if your action doesn't lead to the result that you want right here and now, you must understand that you have to enjoy the process. He, who does, sooner or later will get and will get a lot. You have to do it. Once again, you must understand for yourself clearly, "What do I want?". "What do I have to do to get what I want?" This has to become a basic rule for you: "I WANT, I DO, I GET." You don't have to ask yourself, "Why? What will happen?"

What do I want? What do I have to do to make it happen? Go down this simple path. It's very easy and very effective.

I hope you take this simple rule very seriously. But at the same time, as practice shows, this simplicity very often ends up somewhere in guys' notes and doesn't directly transition to actually doing "I WANT, I DO, I GET" by these rules and canons.

I'M ENJOYING

It's a basic and very necessary thing in order to have success with girls, and for you to get things done effectively. We're going to review the rules, principles, and beliefs that are necessary if we want to get what we want from the opposite sex with maximum efficiency. We're going to talk about emotions.

I thought for a long time about what to call this chapter. "Never Be a Dull Shit" was on my mind. In the end, I decided to call it "I'M ENJOYING." On the principle of "I WANT, I DO, I GET".

I think you've seen (at least once) the "SpongeBob" cartoon? That's an odd question. Nevertheless, there is a lot to learn from this character. How positive this character is, how he faces all problems and difficulties with a smile and constantly continues to be in a state of total enjoyment. This is something you can take from him. That is a very important quality for a seducer.

I have been in training men for many years. I have done a huge amount of group training and individual online coaching. Every day, I face some problems and situations that occur in the lives of dozens of men. It's possible to collect statistics during this time about what qualities are necessary and which ones give results. Guys, who are really good with girls, have one distinctive feature. They act as a battery in any situation, no matter what kind of company they are in: with their friends or at work, they try to meet or sit on a date, they act as a battery. They are willing to share their emotions. Such a guy is not a dull shit who sits in the corner and just waits for an opportunity to show himself.

You just have to look at the nonverbals of a guy like that. The way he sits, the way he smiles, the way he looks and gives his energy. The topics he brings up and the way he speaks, it feels like he's sharing, not taking away. These are the kind of people you really want to connect with. That's the kind of person you're drawn to.

You can make the following analogy. When you look out the

window and there's gray, slushy weather, you don't want to go out there. But when it's sunny and warm outside, you want to go out. It's the same with people. People tend to be drawn to these guys. This is a great quality, which is necessary if you want girls to be attracted to you and look forward to the next date with you after the first one.

I know a huge number of different quotes and beautiful expressions (I don't use them on purpose). Believe me, at one time, I also read all sorts of beautifully written quotes and excerpts from books. It's all a pretty wrapper. So, I want to convey the message to you in simple words, which I hope will strike a chord. In your heart, in your brain, wherever you want. Maybe it will set your thinking and actions on the right course because it's really important.

Maybe you have a job that involves communicating with people, or you used to act in theater plays. But now you're used to having excess energy that you were sharing with others earlier.

Let's make an analogy with a gym so that you understand what I'm talking about. If a guy had been regularly (several times a week) going to the gym to work out for a long time (several months). And then, for whatever reason, he had a lot of work and decided to watch movies instead of going to the gym. Then, in about 10 days, his body started demanding physical activity. The same situation is true for our emotions.

If you're not used to radiating positivity 90% of the time, and you act like a dull shit, then you can't approach a girl and magically become a positive, fun, and cool guy. You can play that, but you're probably going to play it off-key. Especially if it's a date. That's why it's better if you're really that guy, not just seem like it.

In real life, each of us can feel completely different emotions. I can be in an angry mood too. I can have an argument with someone on the street or at work, and it takes me a while to get over it. We all have problems of some kind. Business problems, family problems, someone has health problems. We can feel all kinds of emotions. The question is what percentage of those emotions are some kind of constant negativity (especially if there are no serious reasons for that). If you stay positive only half the time, that's bad, that's not normal. If the ratio is 90% to 10%, for example, 90% of the time, you're positive and 10% of the time, you have a headache or your shoes are rubbing you sore, so you're upset. We can allow ourselves to feel emotions, that's okay. Only crazy people have a mood like a straight line.

Most of the time, you have to be positive. And to keep it that way all the time, you have to train yourself to give emotions. You can enroll in acting classes. There you have to perform on stage to force out emotions. If you have five classes a week, you will force that emotion out of yourself five days a week. On the sixth day, your body will want you to do it. If you don't have time, money, or you don't have anything like that in your town, you can take some text (with a range of emotions in it) and read it yourself, declaim, and record yourself on a voice recorder or on tape. And you'll get used to what you're giving. You can already (even if it's not peculiar to you) add communication with people to your life; where you take the initiative, where you take the first step yourself, and where actions depend on you.

You go to a café, and when you order coffee, you can ask the waiter, "Very few people are here today. Is it always like this on Wednesdays, or just today?" and he'll say something. You can ask something else. If it's a girl, compliment her. And little by little, it will all build up like a snowball.

Let's talk about the second thing you should do. Actions build up character. Act like you're already that positive, cool dude. He tends not to whine about his problems in public, but brings up only positive topics of conversation and tries to bring up negative topics as rarely as possible. There's no point in making people feel sorry for you. You need to bring up topics that make everyone smile.

Forbid yourself to whine or tell someone something bad. To write, God forbid, to some girl or friends: "I'm so tired, I work all the time" and so on. No. Write something good, maybe something good happened yesterday. Write a girl that you're looking forward to the weekend to see her. There are a bunch of variations, which will work for you. If you do it a few times here today, you will be repaid in a couple of days. Do the right thing now, and that's what you'll become. By doing these things, you will become a man with an attitude. Control what comes from you, what you radiate. There must be a minimum of negativity.

When you force yourself to radiate positive vibes, you'll quickly come to the point where your energy will be flowing over the edge. Enjoy your life. When you're on a wave of positivity, you enjoy what you do. Everything that happens in your life should be completely under your control. This way, it's much easier to find a reason to be happy. For some, it's easy and intuitive. If it doesn't work, keep a diary and write five things you're proud of every day. These can be topics of conversation with your friends or your girlfriend on a date. For example, you went to work out, did that many push-ups. Made a new deal. Were afraid to call, but pulled yourself together and did it. Went to a new event you had never been to. Took some guitar lessons, as you've been wanting to learn to play for a long time. If you take notes, it will have a good impact on how you can radiate more positive energy and not radiate negative energy. The right mindset will follow. It will really, really affect the effectiveness of your dating, even the effectiveness of meeting girls.

If you think you're going to be able to play a fun guy, and yet humbly walk down the street with the "how much I hate everybody" look, you're deeply mistaken. It's all noticeable and very often can be felt. Control your emotions. Manage your emotions. Be positive and enjoy your life. It will really help you in all areas of your life.

HOW TO LEARN TO SAY "NO"

Let's talk about a very important rule, which is the ability to say no.

A huge part of the problems men have in communicating with the opposite sex arise because they are afraid, they don't know how to say "NO" to a woman. But it just has to be done.

Let me give you an example from a TV show. A girl comes to a guy, gives him a bracelet, and says, "This is my gift, and I want you to wear this bracelet the whole evening today". He responds with a smile and appreciation, "Thank you so much for the bracelet, but I'm not going to wear it. In my mind, it's too much. I don't want to wear it and I don't have to". Here's another situation. A girl wants to ask a guy out on a first date. He says: "Thank you for the offer, but I'll refuse for now. I'm not ready to promise you that I'll say yes. I need to think about it for a while." At that point, she was expecting a "YES" from him, and she got a "NO" in response.

And rightly so. Because he may have had other plans at that moment. And he, with all his wishes and her expectations, was ready to say "NO". This is commendable and should be adopted.

Men are often afraid to say "NO" in communication, relationships, and seducing women. They are afraid to say "NO" to their friends, parents, relatives, colleagues. Many people have this problem. Some men say "YES" to everything. Whatever you ask him to do; even if he doesn't want to do it, he will comply with your request.

You really should say "NO" to a woman sometimes. After accepting rejection from you, she will be drawn to you even more and will see you as a cooler dude. Of course, we're talking about adequate situations and adequate things.

Think back to the last time you said "NO" to a girl.

Here are a few real-life situations. As a rule, men with all the reasons to say "NO" are afraid to say it. For example, a guy is in a relationship with a girl. He goes out with friends to watch soccer, and she says to him, "Honey, darling, sweetheart, take me with you, so I don't get bored." He realizes that his friends will think that he's an idiot for bringing a girl into a men's company. He wanted to talk alone with his friends, just in a men's company. Even if you love a person, it's okay to take a little break from your sweetheart. But he says, "Yes, of course, honey. Get dressed, let's go".

You start dating a girl, and you have, like, a beard or stubble. And you like it. But she says, "You know, I don't like it. Shave it off". But you like it. However, you comply, you don't say anything, go ahead and shave it off. Even though you could have said, "NO, I like the beard. Why should I change anything?"

Or she doesn't go with you to your friends, but "brainwashes" you bit by bit. Says that your friends are kind of flawed and leading you nowhere. Look at that one, he has flaws. That friend has those flaws. Her friends are a different thing. So when she goes to a girls' night out with her friends, she says, "Listen, honey, come with me, keep us company. I'm gonna be really scared and uncomfortable without you. Come on, the girls will be very happy." And you imagine all this. You're like in a pigsty, with her stupid friends, who start complaining about life and how they don't get along with guys. After 5-10 meetings, you might even start to like it. You're becoming less and less masculine, but more henpecked. It all begins with your first NO, which you don't say.

Even before the relationship starts, there are a bunch of moments when you just have to say NO as a man. These are moments when you have different desires. When you really don't want to do it. It can be something simple. For example, something like that: the weather outside is hot, but you have agreed with a girl to go on a date, and you say, "Let's go to a café for coffee", but she says, "I do not feel like it, I would go for a walk". That doesn't mean that you have to 100% agree with this desire. If your feet hurt, or you don't like the heat, and you sweat very much, and you're gonna feel embarrassed about that, in that case, you say, "Walking is great, but today we're going to a café, and next time you decide". Take her hand and take her where you want to go. Say

"OK" to all her possible weirdness.

If you do not want to do it, and it's not part of your plans, you should feel free to say "NO". Saying "NO" to women only increases their attraction to you.

Let's review an example when your refusal would look inadequate. For example, you've been dating for a while. You arrive at her house, and at the same time, she receives a large, heavy package that she can't bring into the house. She asks you to help her, but you say "NO". That kind of rejection seems silly.

I hope that most of those, who are reading this book, already understand what is considered appropriate men's behavior.

This is the first step to being able to appreciate and respect yourself. If you are constantly following and indulging other people's desires and not thinking about your desires at all, you will never have 100% respect for yourself. Love yourself and value yourself. If you don't love and appreciate yourself, no one will.

Do not be afraid to say "NO" to women. Do not be afraid to have desires. Do not be afraid to sort out what you want and what you don't want, what is done with pleasure and what is done because you are afraid. You shouldn't do anything out of fear in your life, relationships, or seduction.

STOP FEELING SORRY FOR YOURSELF

A lot of people don't want to admit the simple fact that in our society, it is fashionable and popular to dramatize and suffer.

I once bought a T-shirt, tried it on, but it didn't fit me. It fit me small. I'm not going to wear that T-shirt. I'm not going to cry because it's not my size. I'm going to send it back and buy myself a T-shirt in my size. I'm not going to make a tragedy out of it. I will not, on a daily basis, wear this T-shirt and walk around in it and look like an idiot.

A lot of people will say I'm a cynic. How can you compare people's feelings and relationships, to clothes. Do you really mean to say that a girl, is just a thing, or a girl should treat a man like a thing. No. But a lot of people could use a similar attitude about dealing with the opposite sex.

If, it's not your thing. If, it doesn't suit you. If, it makes your life uncomfortable, or you hoped for one thing, but it didn't work out. Don't make a big deal out of it. Pick up a T-shirt in your size. Pick a t-shirt that fits you and in which, you'll feel like all 10 out of 10 points, not make it, a super event. Don't bring emotion into your life just because it didn't turn out the way you wanted it to.

I'll give you some real life examples. When attracting drama and tragedy into your life, ends very badly. Unfortunately, the most revealing facts, I can not tell because of the fact that very many things that happen in life in men, works the principle of confidentiality.

For example, there was a story when a girl leaves a guy, (just disappears on his birthday), and she goes with some other, to rest at the resort. And he, instead of telling her to fuck off and do something interesting and useful for himself. He goes out on the cold stairs and drinks wine on the cold stairs. You ask why? Why not drink in the apartment? It's warmer, it's got a comfortable couch. Because it's more tragic on the stairs. He might have seen it in a movie, where they showed him that it's fashionable, it's healthy, it's great.

If a guy is in love with some girl and God forbid, the love is unrequited. He starts to wind himself up. He begins to sit by the window, to try on a mask that his life is not working out the way he wants it to. He suffers, he worries, he thinks about her all the time, and it ends very, very badly.

I was once approached by a guy who had been in love with a girl for 15 years, (just think about that phrase), 15 years. Every time she started dating someone and even got married and then divorced, he waited. He hoped, he believed, that the next guy who showed up in her life would soon disappear. And after that, she would pay attention to him. For 15 years, his life had been a complete piece of shit. You think he didn't know or didn't understand that it was possible to live differently. He knew and understood, but he showed everyone, his parents, his friends, everyone around him how fucked up his life was. He told it to everyone, at every meeting of his friends, and every year he had fewer and fewer friends. He was trying to get the story out there to show, "Look guys, my life is so miserable. What are you guys talking about? Soccer or a new episode of a series. It doesn't matter. I'm in unrequited love. Let's talk about that. Why are we talking about it for only half an hour? Let's talk some more." No one is interested.

People I knew (a guy and a girl), they were in a relationship. The relationship sucked. They were on and off. Finally they split up, for a longer period of time. The girl starts sleeping on the floor, suffering, not washing, not eating. When you see her, she speaks in a voice as if she is about to die. She, tries to convey to everyone, to show that she is suffering.

Where does that come from? Don't you understand; if you get the idea that you want to suffer, you have to dismiss that thought instantly. If you suffer, you're a complete idiot. No one will suffer with you, and they don't want to hear about it. No one will consider you a normal girl or a normal guy when you start sharing your suffering about a relationship.

I totally understand (God forbid anyone) people who suffer

because of a relationship where everything was cool, healthy, everything was great. And then, for example, someone gets a terminal illness, and the relationship ends there. Someone passes away or gets in a car accident. Before that, that relationship was great, but then, that person disappears from life. It's really very difficult. This is a situation where you can cry and suffer. It takes, a very long time to get out of it.

But when it comes to falling in love. When, you've either had nothing at all, or you've had a few encounters. Or you had a shitty relationship where you were constantly quarreling, fighting and cheating on each other, you were going over and over in your head whether or not this person was right for you. And after that relationship started not working out, you start crying or suffering. Stop it. Don't allow yourself to do that, no way. It's not healthy, it's not fashionable.

In practice, I've seen people whose suffering turned into a psychological illness. Very often, such thoughts and such attitudes to the process of building relationships and building a personal life end in schizophrenia. A guy falls in love with a girl, she does not respond the way he would like her to (the T-shirt does not fit) and he begins to think even more about it. He starts painting certain pictures in his head of how things are going to be okay with them. And then, at some point, he starts having voices in his head that say, "You'll be fine, everything will be great. Write or call her." It ends very badly. There are a lot of people like that, a lot of people.

I'm pretty sure there are no such people among your acquaintances. But there are a lot of cases like this. Even if your life doesn't have one, you can open the scientific literature and read about the causes of schizophrenia. That's one of the points.

Why does this happen? Because at just the right moment, instead of saying to yourself, "I did the best I could. I asked her out, I tried different approaches, but it didn't work." It's like with the T-shirt. What can I do to have a cool T-shirt? Buy it and try it on. If it fits me and I look great in it, walk around in it. If you buy it, try it on and it doesn't fit you, buy another one, until eventually you find the shirt you feel great in. If in communicating with some girl, you still don't feel awesome. You don't feel the way you want to feel. You don't have to cry and suffer.

Very often, in counseling sessions with me, men cry (it's not because I'm bringing them to tears) it's because when they tell their story, they're worried about the girl not going on a third date after the second two. These are men in their 40s, not 18 year old guys, but men in their 30s and 35s. They're crying because some girl didn't accept a bouquet of flowers from him or because she cheated on him twice. He wanted to forgive her, but she told him to fuck off. He cries instead of saying to himself, "This is some bullshit going on. Why would I want this, I don't want this. It's not right for me," and calmly move on.

Never allow any drama into your life. In no way, don't try to show how you're suffering because of the end of the relationship. No one needs that. If you have a desire for someone to feel sorry for you and hear about your pain, and you sit at a meeting with friends with a "sour face" and say that you don't want anything to eat or drink. And you want them to ask what's wrong with you. Throw that away - fuck it. Put a fake smile on your face and get some work to do.

When you have plenty of free time and nothing to do, you'll start (even if you're in a great relationship), at some point, making up different stories. Screwing yourself up. You start writing something to your Friends. Depression sets in. You make up problems for yourself, so you start having relationship problems.

Guys and girls, even in the dating phase, when things don't work out, start thinking suicidal thoughts. Imagine not fitting a T-shirt, and instead of buying another T-shirt, jumping out the window. If you've done all you can do and didn't get what you expected; the whole world is open before you. There are a lot of people with whom you have a much happier story waiting for you. You don't have to dwell and suffer about it. You don't have to cry into your pillow, you don't have to cry on the shoulder of your friends, your parents. You don't have to cry at all. You have to say to yourself, "I did everything I could. I've moving on." And that's the right attitude, that's the right position, that's the right behavior for a man.

When you're suffering and crying into your pillow, you shouldn't expect compassion from those around you. You're doing a fucked up thing.

Don't be dramatic and don't bring the fashion of suffering into your life and you'll be fine.

THE MAIN RULE OF LIFE

I am often asked the question. How do you build a happy relationship?

But in order for you to have a happy relationship, you need to initially build yourself. You need to build yourself as a person, then all you have to add to that, is the right choice. The right choice of a girl. You'll have a happy, harmonious relationship. You will have the kind of relationship that many will call perfect.

But how do you do that? What might you be missing? Why, some men get to build relationships and be happy and successful through life, and others, get absolutely nothing. What is the difference between them? The difference is life rules and beliefs. Take the life rules and beliefs of this man who did well, apply them to your life and make them your own, and your life will start to change. Life will begin to change, events in life will begin to change, and everything will be okay.

Today I want to tell you about one of my biggest rules in life. It's: "If you leave, leave." That's a real problem for modern men, a real pain. Even now, there are many times when men behave contrary to this rule and it gets them in trouble. What is this rule about? What does it say? What does it teach? What does it form?

First: It shapes thinking before you open your mouth. Think before you make a decision, not afterwards. That rule is that if you tell your girlfriend, your wife, "we're breaking up," that means the story is over, period. No comebacks. No, "And I've been thinking about it and I've decided I've overreacted." If you say that phrase (we're breaking up), the story is over forever. In the future, you can draw conclusions from this story. You will apply those conclusions to the next story with another girl. You don't take a step back to go back to the way things were. Are you just starting some story with a girl, something didn't go according to plan? Delete the chat room, block her, then panic, then after a day, two, a week unblock her; and try to pretend nothing happened and text her all the time. Expect trouble if you behave that way. You and the girl have some sort of micro conflict and you say, "That's it, we're breaking up. I'm leaving." But, in fact, you expect her to stop you and as soon as, she stops you, you instantly change your behavior. That is, you say one thing and you do another. So your life will change for the worse if that happens. That's not to say any serious things.

You split up today, and then you get back together. One day, you don't fucking need her and she's the worst woman on planet Earth, and the next day, "she's the most beloved." If you triggered the process of that person disappearing from your life, if, you said it out loud, then that's the end of the story. That goes for relationships, it goes for friendships. You don't have to give people a second chance.

If you've said some words, you don't have to back down. It's going to lead to you, being very careful about those words. You will do things in your life in a measured way. It will lead to the fact that those people who will be around you will understand very well that you are not a person to whom you can "shit on your head" endlessly, and you will turn a blind eye to that. Your life, your character, you will change. If your life rule is "if you leave, you leave," your life will change.

By following that rule, you will take those moments very seriously. You will be very deliberate about the decisions you have in your life. You will understand that if you've done it, you follow through with it. You're categorical about it exactly as much as you need to be. I hope that such a rule will become yours as quickly as possible.

DISCARD EVERYTHING THAT DOES NOT BRING JOY TO YOUR LIFE

We're going to talk about some simple rules and principles. They will help you in your life, communicate better with the opposite sex. This rule is "DISCARD EVERYTHING THAT DOES NOT BRING JOY TO YOUR LIFE." There are some people who do everything to ensure that, such a rule is not followed.

Men, as well as women, try to impose on others; that the more, problematic and difficult relationships you have in your life, the more normal it is. And this applies as much to family, relationships with girls as it does to socializing with friends. The rule of "DISCARD EVERYTHING THAT DOES NOT BRING JOY TO YOUR LIFE" is a very important rule.

Everyone has a favorite shoe. I was walking my dog once. Wore my favorite Converse sneakers. Went a lot of miles in them. Very comfortable and great shoes. Walking in them is a pleasure. But it happens that when you walk not asphalt, your shoes can get a pebble. As soon as a pebble hits your shoe, you walk, you feel nasty, you hurt, and you are uncomfortable. Tell me, please, what will you do with this pebble if it, brings you discomfort, pain? You're going to stop, take the pebble out of your shoe, and throw it away. You don't need it at all. You're not going to put up with that pebble, and you're going to try to find a way to get along with it. When you come home, you're not going to leave it inside, because it's entered your life. You're not going to say, "I can't just pick it up and put it away." That's the kind of principle that's very useful to adopt in your life.

We don't, for some reason, make things easy. We try to make things complicated.

If you're in a relationship with a girl (no matter what stage it is) you just slept with her or maybe you've been married for years, the stage is unimportant. In your relationship, you constantly start to have problems of some kind, which brings you a lot of trouble, worries, and you feel uncomfortable. For example, because of a relationship with a girl, you start drinking alcohol or smoking weed. What is the reason for this? If before, you didn't have these problems. The reason for all of this, your relationships. They make you worse and don't bring you joy. You can't sleep well at night. You're constantly worried and can't focus on important things. Problems in business or work begin and you, everything falls apart.

If you're in a relationship that causes you (like a pebble that brings you discomfort) to be on the verge of a psychological breakdown, you need to realize that you don't need that kind of girl. You don't want a girl who makes you feel like crap all the time. You don't want a relationship that makes you feel guilty.

If you're in a relationship where you constantly feel guilty, feel like a loser, and so on, then you need to do something. It's a sign that this is not yours and you, don't need it.

This rule doesn't just apply to your life where you're dating a girl, but also to your family and friends. Look at who you're friends with? If that friendship doesn't bring joy, doesn't bring positive emotions, why is he in your life? Even worse if you have a misunderstanding. You said the wrong thing, he got offended or you looked the wrong way, and so on. In your life, you don't fucking need people like that.

A very important principle about relationships is, "Relationships are easy or nothing." If you think it's bullshit. That relationships can't be easy, and you can't get high in a relationship, and it's work. That friendship is a job. Then why would you want that kind of relationship? Why would you want a friendship where you have to work and you can't get high and you can't be yourself? You're supposed to enjoy a relationship where you can relax 100 percent and have fun.

If you're in a relationship that lasts a few months or a few years. You're staying late at work so you don't have to go home, and you're spending time with people who are strangers to you because at home, you don't feel comfortable. You have huge problems. What's the reason for that? Who is the reason for this? Does that reason have a name? If your discomfort, your unhappiness, your grief has a name, fuck it up.

You need to attract people (this goes for relationships and friends) who will give you a sense of joy, positivity. If that's not happening, why do you need it? Throw out people who don't bring you positive, joyful emotions. It makes a huge improvement in your life. That's one piece of advice I wish I'd given myself before I was 25. Communication with a certain person doesn't bring you joy? Throw it away, like that one pebble. Surround yourself with people who will bring you joy in communication and with whom you will feel happy. You have to follow these rules and live by these rules. If you don't, your life won't change.

THE MAIN SECRET OF MALE HAPPINESS

Unfortunately, a huge percentage of modern men do not even know it exists.

But I want to start with a little riddle. Let's imagine a situation where there is a guy and a girl. The guy wants to develop the story, the events with this girl, but he has only two options. There are no other options.

Option one. To buy the latest model of iPhone for yourself, your favorite. Use it for yourself and keep it for yourself.

Option two. Buy this iPhone as a gift, and as a gift to give this girl. How do you think, in which of these options the probability of development of history between them is higher? Bad news if you chose the second option. Bad news if you think he should give the phone to her as a gift.

The main secret to male happiness is, "Invest in yourself, not in women."

I'm not talking about iPhones, I'm talking about working on your knowledge. I'm talking about working on your communication skills and your financial success. About your attractiveness, both physically and in terms of style. Working on your health, setting accomplishments and goals. Work on your self-esteem and self-love. Work on all of these points and you'll do great with women.

If a man thinks that if he, will be solving problems for a woman, forgetting about solving his own problems, and she will end up with him? No. She, at some point, will look at you and say you're nothing. She'll see how troubled you are.

If you think you're going to shower the girl with gifts and you can't afford to dress normally, she'll be with you, you're very wrong. If it's a choice between giving her perfume or buying a new perfume for yourself, you should buy it for yourself. If it's a choice between listening to her whine or working on your goals, you should work on your goals. These situations are all too common.

When a guy first meets a girl and she sees him as "free ears" she starts telling him how someone doesn't understand her and what a tough day she's had. He listens to her for an hour a day, two hours a day, three hours a day. With all that, he's not growing as a person at all. He thinks that if he pleases her, if he gives her what she wants at the moment, she will be with him in the end. No. When she gets a little tired of him as a free psychologist, she'll tell him, "You're nothing." The best thing a guy should say to her is, "Look, I'm sure you can handle it, but I have a lot to do."

If you've promised yourself you're going for a run right now, then do that instead of texting her. You have to be very aware that even if you want to develop a story with her, you need to invest in yourself. You need to work on yourself. Because when a man, thinks that if he, will adjust to a girl's schedule (thereby forgetting his business, his plans) and she will end up with him, that's not true. It doesn't work that way.

If you think you're going to live her dreams and her goals (forgetting about your dreams and forgetting about your goals), she's going to stay with you because of that, and realize how awesome you are and love you, appreciate you, and so on. No. Because when you give up your goals, you become nothing. In the end, she won't want to build a relationship with an empty space.

The man who runs out on a date with a huge bouquet of flowers is often dressed just awful. He spends money, on that huge bouquet of flowers and yet, realizes he's going to have to save money for the next week. That's terrible. It's not right. It's never, ever going to get him results. Invest in yourself, not in women. It makes a very serious difference in the way you think.

When you work on yourself. When you invest in yourself. You start to really understand your value. You don't have this mindset that: "if I come in without a gift, I'll be bad for her." When you have a few points on which you know you're awesome, she's going to reach out to you. She will want to develop a relationship with you.

So if you want to get to the level of true male happiness, invest in yourself. An investment in yourself, stays with you forever. An investment in yourself, stays with you forever. An investment in a woman is unselfish in nature. When she sees that your investment in her has dried up, she will look at you and see that you are a nothing and leave you. You will regret that all this time, you spent your energy on her and not on yourself.

For yourself, you are the most important and most beloved person on this planet.

CHAPTER 2: VALUABLE SKILLS BEFORE YOU START DATING

The Rule Of Three "No's"

Many guys say that after a date, the girl says, "Let's stay friends." Or they can't get through to the girl. Many don't understand why this happens. There can be many reasons. Any little thing plays a role. What are you talking about? How do you behave?

I want to talk about something that is very, very important. What's the difference between meeting and dating? A lot of guys think that it's enough to come on a date, talk for an hour or two, and it should, it will work itself out. And a few days later, you're going to have sex.

During communication and your meeting, if you act like an interesting conversationalist, she will only see you as an interesting conversationalist. If you want her to get a sexual desire for you, you have to do things. You have to do things that will position you as a man that she will have sex with.

Take one simple rule for yourself: any encounter with a girl, must contain at least three NO's. Three times, she has to stop you doing the action. For example, you are sitting with her in a cafe and at one point, try to hug her. To this she says, "Look, you're in a hurry, let's not be in a hurry. We just met and this is our first meeting." She takes your hand away. That's the first "NO."

You continue your communication further and after a while, put your hand on her leg. She will react normally at first, but you begin to raise your hand higher and higher. She says, "Wait. You're in too much of a hurry" and takes your hand away. That's a second "NO."

You try to kiss her. She may look away. That's your third "NO."

Three actions, in a man-woman format. You hit on her. You

hug her. At least three "NO's" you have to do. Now, it will not be a meeting, but a date. The girl will go home and realize that this is the man she is going to have sex with. She will never say, "Let's stay friends." She won't see you as a girlfriend, an interesting conversationalist, a psychologist. She will see you as a potential man. Act on the first date.

THREE MESSAGES THAT YOU SHOULD NEVER SEND TO A GIRL

This includes situations where you have met a girl and maybe even went on a date and decide to start corresponding with her a few days after the date. Also, this applies to the situation when you want to meet on a dating site or on social networks.

I understand that sometimes nothing comes to mind. I understand that it's hard to get creative with something, but if suddenly, you don't know what to write it's better to sit and think. But don't do that and don't write the kind of posts I describe. Because, this is the very real disease. There is a huge percentage of men who send messages like this.

Message #1. "Hi!" and that's it. The guy sends this message to the girl and waits. I don't know what he's waiting for. In the most awesome and best-case scenario, she'll reply back with "Hi!" too. That's fine if you're talking on the walkie-talkie. When you need to make sure someone on the other end can hear you. But, in the real world, your " Hi!" message, it's infuriating. That message, it doesn't make you want to text you back. If you think that by texting just "Hi!" she'll instantly start responding to you (to a guy she doesn't know), she won't. It doesn't work that way. With a message like that you're antipathy towards yourself. By such a message, you cause unwillingness to communicate with you. So, by no means send such a message. It's not a problem if you start your correspondence with this word, but it shouldn't be your only message. For example, "Hi!" and some question. "Hi!" some question and interesting, funny information.

Message #2. "What do you do?" A variation of this message, "How are you? What's up? What are you doing?"

It feels like you're sitting at home on the couch and you're bored. You have an uninteresting life and you decide, out of boredom, to wonder "What does a girl do?" If you add, " Hi! What are you doing?" then that message is no good. You don't have to get too clever. Think like chess, two moves ahead. Think about it, when a girl gets this message, what exactly is she supposed to answer? That she's sitting at home, watching YouTube, or out with friends. And then what? Answer, what's next?

If you want to chat with a girl about how either of you are spending your time. It's better if you write a funny story or a funny interesting incident. That way you'll encourage her to write about what's going on in her life. Such a message will trigger her emotions, and those emotions will help, increase her desire to text with you. When a girl gets the message, "What are you doing?" she catches a facepalm. She thinks, "You're serious. That's the best you could come up with? That's the best thing you could have written?" Do you think a question like that helps communication? No. Don't do that on a date, either.

Message #3. My favorite message of all time. The cherry on the cake. Sending an audio message.

When is it okay to send a girl an audio message? If you, have hands, then you don't. You're not allowed to send audio messages. If you're already hooking up and you have a relationship, you haven't seen each other in a while, and you start exchanging voicemails, pictures for a change of correspondence, that's fine. But if you're the first to send an audio message, especially when you're trying to get to know her online. What are you counting on? Why are you doing it? Why are you sending your audio message? You don't have to do that.

Don't do all three of the options I've described, under any circumstances. Sit down and think about it. Write something simple and easy. But, by no means so tedious and stressful.

How To Start A Texting With A Girl? How To Properly Flirt With A Girl In Correspondence? Examples.

If you want online dating to develop into a real, full-fledged, live date, you need to make it easy to communicate with you in this text message. It should be interesting, there should be a sense of humor and, of course, there should be flirting. Then the likelihood that a date will happen will grow exponentially.

For example, you can send a message like this: "Hi! What number should I call/text to ask you out?

90% of girls will write their number right away. Others offer to text first, and then give your phone number.

You can write the simplest message, "Hi! How are you feeling?" But it's better to come up with a more creative one.

Before you write the first message to a girl, look at her profile, photos and description. You might be able to find something interesting to help you come up with a message.

If the girl has pictures from other countries, you can, use that. For example: " Hi! Do you like to travel to warm countries, too?". Or if she doesn't have a description and you can't write your own message linking it to her photos. For example: "Hi! You haven't written anything about yourself. You're a mystery girl." If you began to correspond, then you can try to invite her to a meeting. For example: "I would love to solve you. Let's meet and have coffee and get to know each other better."

Don't be afraid to flirt and write ambiguities. Hopefully, you're not just starting a correspondence with one girl, but several. Because, not all girls will respond to your messages. Others won't respond the way you'd like them to. But you don't have to stop, but keep moving forward.

HOW TO GET OUT OF THE FRIEND ZONE

Sometimes it happens that a girl has sent you into a friend zone. But here is a very important point: no one can send you into a friend zone unless you want them to. If in your reality, the friend zone is something horrible and bad, then sending you into it is impossible.

Why do some guys end up in a friend zone? Why do they have a format with a girl they like where there is only friendship? It's all about when a guy starts communicating with a girl, he likes her, but she starts slowing down the communication, hinting and promoting the friendship theme. In his reality, friendship is good, it's okay.

When you communicate with a friend, you will tell him how much you like her, what a perfect friend you are, how much you do for her, what a kind, good boy you are. But she doesn't do anything and nothing is moving for you. You're going to say that to get your friend to support you. And because he's your friend, he'll say words of encouragement that everything will work out, everything will work out, everything will be fine.

But really, your friend won't say that at this point, he treats your behavior as shameful. And your actions are likely to resemble those of a lowlife.

You can give up on your friend or replace him or her. And say that everyone doesn't understand you and how the world works. But the problem, is that the girl you're friends with and you have a friend zone, she also treats you like a lowlife. She thinks you're nothing. Your behavior, shows that you like her. And that you're willing to accept this friendship format and sit on the bench.

You can tell and tell everyone that she writes or tells you that you're the best man she's ever had in her life. She can say, "How great is this. I'm thankful to God that you came into my life, thankful to fate."

I'll tell you, that's just a manipulation you fell for. She doesn't see you as a man. She has no feelings for you. She's using you and at your expense, boosting her self-esteem. Or she just uses your "free ears" to tell you her problems. And you, because you're afraid of losing her, become more and more supportive and tell her how cool she is.

In some formats, this comes across as mercurial. She might use you as a cab driver. Or begging for gifts all the time. Some guys, lending money for this. A girl uses you in the guise of friendship.

You think that every day, it gets better, and a little more and you, start dating her. But in fact, you are wildly mistaken and wrong. Because, with each passing day, she becomes more and more convinced that you are nothing.

Imagine sitting with her and you think everything is super and everything is blooming and smelling. But in reality, you're in a cesspool. She's looking down on you and watching you sit there completely in feces. You think she's still going to look at you and see how great you are. But the truth is, your life is terrible and she looks at you like you're nothing. Every day and every month, she sees less and less of you as a man. Less and less of a prospect that there could be anything with you.

Now let's imagine there's a guy. And he looks at this format of communication in the form of a friend zone, not as something wonderful, but as a big problem. He's going to get out of there.

If, all of a sudden, you're in a friend zone, the only possible course of action is to go all-in. Start seducing her and act not like a friend, but like a man who goes all in. Either you succeed, or you stop communicating with her forever.

You ask her a date. You try to kiss her. If you make out with her at your house, try having sex with her. If you go through these steps, you're out of the friendship zone forever. Friendship is out of the question when you meet her like that.

If suddenly, at any stage, you start to get stuck again, and something does not work out, you should not want to remain her friend. In no case, don't even allow a moment, about going back to her. That's what it is, all or nothing.

Therefore, a normal, cool man who respects himself will not

be in a friend zone. Even if you are there now, but you didn't know this information, get out of there as soon as possible. Here and now, start to get out of there. Start to get out, so you don't end up there again. Do what depends on you. Be what happens. You'll either have some kind of relationship with her, like a girl, like a man with a girl, or you'll have nothing.

In fact, friendship and friend zone, it's not zero, it's much worse. It's shameful behavior that should not be allowed in your life. And I hope that you, starting now, fundamentally change the way you look at the friend zone and your friendship with a girl.

If you have a friend zone, you have to persevere, and fast, and start seducing that girl. I hope it works out for you. I hope you can get out of the friend zone.

GIRL'S PARENTS

I want you to succeed. But there is a problem. The problem is that many men, don't understand what that happiness should look like and don't want to put a little effort into it.

I want to talk about the relationship with the girl's parents. One of your criteria when building a relationship and moving into a more serious stage of a relationship, should be how great your communication with her parents is shaping up to be. How on the same page you are, and how you feel warmth, care, and attention from them. That's very important.

It's very important because, unfortunately, a lot of men take it for granted. You don't have to be on knife-edge with her parents. They shouldn't, wipe their feet on you.

I want to talk to you about a few things. One: The expectation of reality. Think about what do you expect? You can write out on a piece of paper how you see communicating with the girl's parents. What emotions do you want it to be? What should it all look like? How you spend time together and how good or not you feel together? You have to imagine what you expect. This is very important.

Some men have no expectations. They live their whole lives in some strange reality, and take it for granted. Others, they have that expectation, but later on, they find that the reality doesn't match their expectation and the reality is much worse. They begin to try on the role of the victim. It's as if someone is forcing him or her to put up with all of this to continue to build this relationship. No one is forcing you. I want you to have that expectation, so that you understand how much of a right this relationship is for the future, if the reality, doesn't match up.

You're going to have to talk to your girlfriend about how you see your future in terms of communication with your parents. Because, there are your expectations and there are her expectations. Some people get in the process of building a relationship, figure out what everyone's expectations are. Some need to sit down and communicate. How often do you communicate with your parents, how often do you communicate with her parents? How much do you listen to their opinions? How can this be improved? You have to sit down and talk it out before you move into a more serious stage of the relationship. Maybe the girl's expectations are completely different from yours.

You can find a girl with parents with whom you will share a team spirit. Who you will want to spend time with, and you will form a family. It's really cool when that's the way it's going to be, not when you have quarrels and you have to prove something, or fit in with someone. Why make peace with it? It's your life.

CHAPTER 3: CONNECTING WITH GIRLS

How To Find A Girl For A Serious Relationship?

If I had to answer this question in one sentence, I would say, "You don't have to look for her.

And now in more detail. You have to be honest with yourself. If you ask a question like that, something in your life is wrong. Very often, men who ask this question, they think that as soon as there is love, as soon as there is a girl, a serious relationship, and you start living together, then you will be happy. That everything will work out for you, and everything will be fine. Let's be honest, that is so not a good life in terms of happiness. Because if you, were doing great right now, you wouldn't be asking that kind of question.

And so a guy who's hungry for a serious relationship goes on a date with a girl. Starts looking at her under the prism of, how fit is she for seriousness, does she want a serious relationship? Or maybe she's easy-going and she's here to have fun. "I don't need that, it's not right for me," he thinks. That's the kind of guy girls see through. Guys like that are so boring that dating brings discomfort. A normal, cool girl, with whom you could really have a cool, good, harmonious, happy relationship, will not want to see you.

Men who are set up for a serious relationship, and who are currently on the prowl, are easy prey for those girls who will agree to go out with them. The main thing for them is to show him what he wants to see. The main thing is to tell him that she too is all right, good and also waiting for a serious relationship. And so, our main hero, like a kind and naive rabbit, begins to build "air castles". He starts going to meetings with this girl, and at this point, she starts pushing her story through. She says, "We can have a serious relationship. We can only be good and great if you do this, this,

this for me."

If you're fixated on building a serious relationship, if you're not in comfort, happiness, prosperity with yourself right now, no girl is going to help you, be really happy. There can't be, two people happy if each of them separately, isn't happy. It doesn't work that way.

So what to do? Naturally, if you, before that, have not communicated with girls in any way, you know very well that if you, will not look for her, how, something will change in your life. There's a very important point here. I'm not saying that you don't need to connect with people. I'm just saying that you need to be as socialized and normal a man as possible. You have to go to meetings and meet girls. You should go on dates, socialize, kiss, have sex, and spend time together with a girl or girls. It's normal, it's male nature. We are drawn to people. We want so much more when we have a free night out. We can go out for a beer with friends, or watch some movie in the cinema. But we're drawn to women and we don't get enough of that. You go out to meet a girl, to have pleasure. The best, the most wonderful, the strongest relationships, didn't start from the position of, "There's something wrong in my life and as soon as I find a girl, for a serious relationship, things will get better." No. You go on a date with a girl to have a good time. And you, a day later, two days later, maybe three, think about meeting up again. You have to go to the meeting, without any super plans for the future. This applies after two, three, four, and even after five, maybe ten meetings. You just enjoy what's going on.

Three things when looking for a girl for a relationship, for a "healthy person." First: You need to understand who you can consider as a girl for a serious relationship. You have to have criteria. Because, there is a problem in our society. Many men, don't understand what a happy, normal relationship is at all.

For some guys, if a girl cheats with the neighbor, it's normal, and for a family, it's just an extra challenge. Or the girl, doesn't want to do anything and doesn't aspire to anything. Her only goal in life is to find a man who will pull everything himself, and she will be with her friend (maybe even in front of him) calling him names. And for many, that too, is the normal format of a relationship. "She's a woman, it's my responsibility as a man." It's not normal. There are dozens of examples like this.

You have to understand what a serious relationship is. What life values, principles, credo this girl should have. What she is (even before she met you). This is normal. The criteria must be understood.

Second: lead a normal life. If you live as a hermit, if you live by the principle: work home, work home. And your only communication is to talk to the cashier when she asks: "Do you want a bag?" You're not going to get very far that way. You need to communicate with people. You need to talk to girls. You need to meet them and go out with them. So you can choose.

Therefore, you have to have a position that you have something going on. Do as much as you can, live it. Fill your life with those events that will make you happy even without a serious relationship. You should have an interesting, bright, wonderful life. Sometimes, it's a life you can share with someone else. And then, you can add a happy person and together, you will create two, happy, wonderful people. You will be a super team.

Imagine where two people, play tennis. If one player plays okay and the other can barely walk, together, they're not going to strive to win. One can't pull it off alone. Each has to be a great, complete player.

Third criterion. It's good and wonderful if those criteria are somehow met. You can be wonderful, kind, responsive funny and you have a sense of humor. But, if that, only shows up after you've known the person for a very long time, (you can't open up to the person right away), you don't get to that stage. It's just the way the world works.

None of us, come from Mother Teresa, to give 25 chances up front. And if someone is going to give you that chance, that girl isn't much of an asset. You and that girl are unlikely to get anything really worthwhile.

So, evolve, work on yourself. Be the kind of person that

people will want to be in a relationship with. Be the kind of man they want to cling to. And when you, find a girl who meets your criteria, you won't have any questions. Get the idea out of your head that you want a serious relationship, here and now.

When you're 27 or 28 and your mom tells you it's time to find a girl for a family. And it's embarrassing in front of your friends. But it doesn't depend on your age or on the events that happened in your life before. Live an interesting, vibrant, rich, social, active life. And then, sooner or later, you'll find that girl with whom, without any additional plans for it, you yourself will want to build a relationship. Everything will work out for you. It will be easy, simple, and most importantly, a happy relationship.

WHERE TO FIND A GOOD GIRL?

Guys often wonder how to find a good girl?

It would seem that the answer to this question is obvious. Let's try to figure out where to find a good girl? The question, of course, is based on various stereotypes.

I would like to start with the word - find. There is some kind of trouble with it. Because, as a rule, this question is asked by guys of two types. The first type: the guy who is 26 years old and single. He doesn't get along with girls. He doesn't have a relationship. He doesn't know what to do about it. Type two: the guy tried to get acquainted, went on a date and if he met a beautiful girl, she was dull and boring very quickly. Or he met a girl with whom he had something to talk about, but her appearance didn't meet his standards. Where to find a beautiful and intelligent?

When you ask the first and second type of guy, "What did you do for this?" The answer you get is, "I went on two dates last year, sweaty, tired, and now, I'm looking for a way to find that perfect girl who will meet all my criteria without stressing." Such guys want to save their energy and to have a girl who is already at hand. With whom, will be a good, wonderful, happy relationship and kept the energy to play in the PlayStation. Not to waste energy on all of these, your seduction, dating, and so on.

On the one hand, it seems like a good aspiration. On the other hand, in life, you can't always enter cheat codes and get what you want without stressing. It doesn't happen that way. You have to understand that if you're wondering where to find a good girl. You have to answer the question, "What did I do to find her?" What effort, did you put in? And very often, that effort is minuscule. If you went on two or three dates, texted two or three girls on tinder, and nothing happens. So the effort you put in is not enough. It's not a sprint, it's a marathon. If you want a girl that fits your criteria (and I'm glad you have them, and you understand that there are girls good and not good, worthy and unworthy), you have to understand that you have to put a lot of effort into this. And don't try to feel sorry for yourself and think that there is a way that you can reach out and she is already yours. It doesn't work that way.

There are no places that will guarantee you that the girl will have a selection of those characteristics and qualities that you dream of. You have to understand, if you go to a strip club, the chance that the girl will be good is small. If you have, one of the criteria you put up for a girl is: empathy or that she's invested in the attitude too, you can go to a volunteer center. With a high probability, the girl will have this empathy, but it doesn't mean that the other qualities she will have that you are interested in. If you're for a healthy lifestyle, you can go to the gym and find a girl there. You'll think, "Here, she's my dream," but who's to say you'll be interested in her. But there's a guarantee that those girls who fit your criteria, who fit the picture you've painted of yourself, are walking down the street. These girls, go to the store to buy clothes, go to the grocery store. Some of them take public transportation. These girls, go to concerts, events. These girls can meet you at any time and in any situation. It can even be a nightclub or a dating site. Because these are people. And each of them has her own story. So, I don't recommend listening to people who say, "I heard that very nice girls, go to the theater."

There was a case where a guy went to the theater a lot, but never got to meet a girl who fit his criteria. But now he hates the theater and wakes up at night in a cold sweat because he was forced to buy another ticket to the theater. There are guys who start out going to dances, but they hate dances and keep going there. They think that's where they'll meet a girl who's athletic and beautiful.

Start getting involved in whatever you want, as long as it gives you an inner feeling of fascination and enjoyment. Find your passion. Start, with the process of dating, looking for a girl who is nice and worthy. Meet everywhere you see a girl you're attracted to. And realize that you need to be like a gold digger, sifting through the sand before you find the gold bullion. If you like a girl, get to know her. On the street, on the Internet, in a store, on the subway, in a nightclub anywhere. You might bump into a girl where you'll know; it's her, or the in-between stage of your life. That, you'll find out in the process. Maybe it will be clear the moment you arrange a date with her, or after the first date, or a week later. You don't have to live under an illusion and you don't have to live under stereotypes that somewhere, there are places where you will get a girl who will be your ideal on a tray. It's not going to be like that.

So, if you have the criteria and you really want to have a decent, good girl next to you. You have to understand that to do this, you have to make an effort. If you make an effort, then everything will happen.

WHAT TO DO AND HOW TO MET A GIRL WHO IS WALKING WITH HER FRIEND?

Much more often you see girls walking in pairs. Anywhere you can meet a girl who is walking with her friend. And it turns out that the guy who has already started somehow, who got over his fears and getting acquainted with girls. He can get her phone number and ask her on a date. But he only does this when the girl goes alone, but when she goes with a friend, it's scary.

But, what's scary about having two of them? What if they physically start hurting you? I hope you're not afraid of that. What's scary is that suddenly, they'll crush you with their morals.

Well, here's the good news. Statistics say that any guy who meets girls that go solo. And the statistics when he starts approaching girls who go together are about the same. Conventionally speaking, there are as many phone numbers per 100 introductions to girls who go alone as there are to 100 approaches to girls who go as a couple.

It's not harder, it's not scarier, it's not terrible. It doesn't undervalue your success or make things harder. With the skills you have, you'll have exactly the same results. You shouldn't be afraid of that.

What is the best way to behave in a situation like this? Some girls may live by the principle "neither to themselves nor to people". For example, there is a girl (usually one slightly prettier than the other), you go to the one who is prettier. The second immediately realizes that it is not her. She understands that today is not her day again. In this situation, aggression can only come from her side if she feels that you are in for the long haul. No one wants to be the third extra.

If you start from afar. Sometimes it's helpful when the introductions last 5, 7, 8 minutes. That's a good thing. You have more time to open up. You have opportunities to prove yourself somehow, and the girl starts to get more used to you. But when you approach two girls, it plays against you. It plays against you in that you might run into negativity from her friend.

If you walk up and she senses that you're a minute, two minutes. You immediately look at the one you like. You ask her name. You say, "Actually, I came up to you because I saw you and wanted to get to know you better somehow, but I see you're busy right now. In fact, I am also in a hurry for an important meeting. I propose to exchange contacts and call you and make an appointment.

When, you start talking and it feels like you're going very fast, you get to the point very quickly. A friend who hears all this, even if she already has some envy inside, she is likely to be silent.

My recommendation. You approach, try to stop them right away and take a number as quickly as possible. Everything will go smoothly enough. Most importantly, you have to remember that there is nothing to be afraid of. Some of the girls, even if you chat longer, won't get in the way. Girlfriends are like that.

Statistics tell us that things happen exactly the same way they do when approaching a single girl. No one has jumped on him yet and no two girls have beaten up any guy when he approached them.

Make your acquaintance. Your fear is not justified. If your fear is not justified, you have to go for it. Make 10 approaches to two girls, and you'll see there's nothing to be afraid of. You can do it on a regular basis. If you periodically see girls who don't go alone, but with their girlfriends, go over and meet them.

HOW TO HAVE A FIRST DATING?

Very often, when guys have had a first date, they think everything was fine. But when you try to call her again, she doesn't answer her calls and messages.

What do you need to do to make first dates so that a girl waits for a second date?

There are a few things I recommend you pay attention to. If you do, the effectiveness of first dates will greatly increase.

First. The problem is that sometimes, a guy on a date really wants a girl to like him. A date is not an exam. My point now; it's very important how you sit, how you communicate, how you relate to what's going on. In a relationship, it should be like this: enjoyment comes first, the experience comes second, and only the result comes third.

Write it out for yourself that you should focus on positive emotions first. Most likely, it will take time for you to really become, behave on dates (especially if you've had few dates and just started your seduction journey) confidently. Sometimes, you'll get hung up on the result. But you have to, reassure yourself. You can reassure yourself that you're here to enjoy the date. Even if it doesn't work out, you become more experienced. As you gain experience, you become cooler. This will help you, as quickly as possible, come to the point where on a date, you're first and foremost, acting natural, relaxed, and buzzed.

When you're nervous and unsure of yourself, it's very much transmitted to the girl. It greatly affects the effectiveness of your date. So, write yourself out somewhere that pleasure comes first. At some points you can pinch yourself to see if you're enjoying yourself. Either you're trying to impose yourself, or you're trying to beg a girl to start looking at you as a more deserving man.

Most guys, when they start getting interested in dating, agonize over the question, what can I talk to a girl about? What topics can you talk about? I think you've heard the information, too, that on a date, there shouldn't be a lot of slack in the dialogue. That is, that there shouldn't be big pauses. Perhaps you've heard that it's better to talk about more positive topics. That is, avoid topics where you complain about something or that involve bad, negative emotions. It's necessary to know that.

It's necessary, but it's not enough. It's good if you, you don't have pauses and your communication goes without slack. But it's much more important how you communicate. And with that, a huge percentage of men have problems. There's no facial expressions, there's no voice acting, there's no gesticulation. It seems that a talking doll sits with the girl. The feeling after such a date is as if you've been in a looking-glass. So you need to work on these things.

If we're talking about facial expressions, when you're telling something that's fun, interesting and dynamic, you can't tell it, it's all with a "sour face."

There are "Hollywood smile" exercises. If you feel like you're having trouble with how emotionally you're speaking, just smile. Try practicing in front of a mirror. Start with that, it's very empowering and will help you a lot.

Speaking of gesticulation. If you came in and folded your arms across your chest and sat in the same pose the whole time, then even if you were telling something interesting, you probably looked like a dull shit. Learn at least one simple gesture. For example, when talking, show your hands and make half-circle gestures (not like a ninja throwing stars). It's much better that way, and it's much more interesting to listen to you than sitting with your hands clasped together. When you're gesticulating during the conversation, it's easier to touch the girl.

Voice. At school, we were told to read more expressively. Expressive means your voice can get louder at certain times and quieter at certain times. If you're communicating as if a train is passing you by, all the sameness, that's not good. You can record your date, listen to how you communicate. That helps a lot. Or turn on the recorder on your phone and tell an interesting story that you often tell on a date or to your friends. Listen to how much your tone of voice changes.

Add to your conversations topics that involve communication between a man and a woman. It could be dating, nightclubs. This dilutes the dialogue. You can talk about learning French and traveling to other countries, that's good too. It shows that you and the girl have intelligence, but it doesn't ignite a spark between you. But when, for example, you talk about dating in nightclubs, and go to the topic of how a woman reacts to a man, in such cases, it will be easier for you to move on to a kiss. It will look harmonious. Therefore, move on to topics of relationships between men and women.

Man, don't be stupid. On the first date, make sure you get stopped at least a few times. I'm talking about physical actions. Not in the sense that you have to list what panties you have at home that your mom bought you and she stopped you from hearing that. No, I'm talking about touching. Or trying to kiss a girl. Preferably three times. If you're insecure, at least once, you should make her stop you. Because, very often, a girl hints to a guy that she's ready now and wants you to kiss, but you won't even try. Therefore, the rule of three NO's. Three times on a first date, she has to stop you. But it shouldn't be that you try to kiss her and she doesn't stop you, then you stop yourself. No. Kiss her.

Don't be afraid to flirt on a date.

Compliments to a girl. What kind of compliments to say? How do you say compliments? Compliments to a girl are the kind you can't say to a man. For example, if we're talking about clothes, you say, "Nice shoes." The same kind of compliment, you might say to your friend or co-worker at work. That's totally normal.

I'm talking about compliments that show you see her as a woman. To a large number of guys, it's very scary to say that on a first date. A small percentage of men dare tell a girl when she comes in with a big cleavage. You might say, "You're making fun of me. Not only will I have to concentrate on the conversation now, but I'll have to constantly lift my gaze higher. If you misbehave, we'll cover it with a napkin." For example, you can compliment her feet. "You have such beautiful legs that your eyes go down on their own." That's something you won't be able to say to a man anymore. And date compliments like "you're so smart," "you're so beautiful," and so on. That's not good for anything. It starts to play against you. So, let the compliments be few, but they will specifically symbolize that you treat her like a man.

No girl comes on a date with the goal of learning something clever. She comes to relax. Maybe you're serious about your studies or you have a business and you're a serious man who's not interested in trivial things. But if you, come in all smart and beautiful and start telling some useful information. For example, why does Catalonia want to secede from Spain? That's educational and good, but it doesn't work. It doesn't increase interest in you.

The most workable topics are the easy ones. They're topics of food, drinking, vacationing outside the city, traveling. These are topics where you laugh, laugh at yourself. Including self-irony helps a lot. So if at some point you get the idea that you've started talking on some really, too smart topics, then say, "Something you and I have started talking on some smart topics today, let's try to be simpler," and switch to a simpler topic.

Another problem I see a lot is the ragged pace. This is when a guy has written out some ready-made questions for himself and starts asking them to the girl. Don't turn a date into throwing a lot of questions at a girl. For example, you ask her, "What kind of music do you like to listen to?" To which she replies: "I like listening to Linkin Park." "I see." "What kind of sports do you like to play?" and so on. If you ask a question, develop the subject. It shouldn't look jerky. If you're bombarding her with questions about music and right away, about sports, about movies, and so on, that's not good. Ask a question, develop the topic. Tell her yourself something related to the topic. Dig deep into the topic. You shouldn't jump from topic to topic. It should all flow smoothly and naturally. You should linger on each topic. If you jump, instantly, from topic to topic, it's a terrible experience. It ruins absolutely everything and can undermine a lot of your virtues.

HOW DO YOU KNOW IF A GIRL LOVES YOU?

Why do I want to talk to you about this? Very often I come across information on the Internet that a real man (if he is real of course) should only love in a relationship. And for a woman, the most important thing is to be loved and it does not matter if she loves in return. A man must love, and what a woman feels about him and how she feels about him is unimportant. And if he suddenly pays attention to this, then he is a "bad man" and he needs to work on himself and his self-esteem. All of this is complete nonsense.

Real, happy relationships are only possible when two people in a couple (man and woman) love each other. So if you're in a relationship with a girl and you've been together for a long time and you realize that she doesn't love you. You don't want that relationship.

It's silly to wonder if a girl loves you, after the first, second, third date. But I'll say it again. If you've been together for a long time and you're thinking about the next step in the relationship (living together or proposing), this is the moment that's very important to you.

There are many different nuances and different moments. I've chosen five signs that you can clearly tell if a girl loves you or not. That's what I want to talk about.

Besides everything else, the most important thing to pay attention to is actions. Words are nothing. If a girl says she loves you and confesses her love, but her actions say the opposite, then you shouldn't care about her words.

Paying attention to the actions, you want to start with the most important. All the main points, they are secondary. Chances are, your life, will not be all sugar. It won't always be good and wonderful. All of us, have difficulties, trials in life. It's at times like these that they are the most revealing.

Let me tell you a little story. A guy starts a relationship with a girl. For several months they are dating. Everything is good and wonderful. The flowers are blooming and everything smells. He thinks he's found the perfect girl. He proposes to her. She says yes. They are a few months in, planning a wedding, but he gets into a car accident. They take him to the hospital. He's in intensive care. The doctors tell him that he won't be able to walk anymore. After that, the girl, never once shows up at the hospital. Not once. And a few days later, his friends, spot her with another guy in his arms in a cafe. She's kissing, laughing, smiling, as if nothing is going on.

A miracle is happening. The main character in this story is doing well. He gets on his feet, in spite of the doctors' diagnosis. He begins to walk. The process of rehabilitation and recovery takes place. He calls her, but she doesn't answer her calls or texts. She blocks him everywhere. Despite, in spite of such an act, in spite of such a reaction. The first thing he does when he gets out of the hospital. He goes to her house to tell her that he loves her. Despite her behavior, he wants their wedding to take place on the scheduled date. This is utter nonsense.

He should be thanking fate for not getting very far with this girl, and wasting just a few months of his life on her. A simple test, where an accident, showed him who was in front of him.

So if you and the girl, together, went through the problems that happened in your life. And with dignity (you and she) behaved in that situation. Then that girl, loves you. She is worthy of being in a relationship with you.

The second thing to pay attention to is fidelity.

How do you react when a girl cheats on you with another guy? I think it's pretty clear to you. Cheating is not forgiven. To cheating, it is impossible to turn a blind eye. Cheating does not tolerate any excuses.

In a relationship, if a girl loves, she won't allow even a hint of her infidelity to you. You won't wonder, "How do you react if she brings a gift from her co-worker?" Or comes home with flowers you didn't give her. She comes home with a bouquet of flowers, you ask, "What is that?" She: "It's some guy who came by. I told him we could only be friends. He's the one who brought the flowers."

Someone drops her off at work. She is texting with someone. Her ex-boyfriend shows up. A childhood friend, invites her over for coffee. In a relationship where a girl loves her man, this is not acceptable. It's not going to happen if she loves you. If moments like that happen, then not even close, not even on the horizon, a normal relationship, with her is not going to happen.

I believe that if you have to explain, such moments to a girl, it means that all is not well in your relationship. When there is a dialogue between you. And you say to her, "If two people love each other, and you come home with a perfume that someone gave you at work. You're hurting me. You make me doubt my feelings for you. This is not acceptable in a normal relationship. If you have to explain this to her and she changes her behavior to you. Then it means that she didn't love you. Whatever she told you. Even though you are having a good time together.

Third point. She constantly emphasizes your flaws.

We are not perfect. Not me, not you. No matter how much you've evolved. No matter how great, cool person you are, we all, have flaws. But when we love, a person (I'm talking about wholesome love), we accept those flaws. We don't try to shake a person's confidence by emphasizing those flaws. We don't try to cause (every day or every week) drama, nagging. We understand that we love the person with their flaws.

If a girl (the simplest example) starts comparing you to another guy. If she, starts telling you, "I need a little different man around. I need a strong man. Why, you're always acting wrong. When are you going to be normal? Why, my friend has a guy who has no problem doing what she wants, and I have to wait for you to do for me what I want?" And so it goes on from day to day. She doesn't love you. Otherwise, there wouldn't be conversations like this.

You have to be clear. Even if you fix in yourself what she wants and your relationship, it will get better. You're dead wrong. Nothing like that is going to happen.

You don't want a girl who is with you and keeps telling you that she will only love you when you change. Not the way you are now, but the way you should be. And once you become that, then you'll be fine. She doesn't love you.

Next point. The girl doesn't value the relationship.

A girl has to understand that her actions (especially weird and inadequate) can affect you to disappear from this relationship. You will end them. At times like this, she sometimes, begins to sacrifice her desires. Maybe even her interests. Which you also need to do.

A simple example. A guy and a girl have been dating for several years. They have a dream, to fly to Bali for a vacation. A good dream. (I want too). The guy, has a job where he can't go away for long. The job isn't remote and he can't take a week, a month off. But it, brings its own benefits. He's in a period where every action he takes in terms of work, brings a good return. But she wants to go. So, this girl, for three months, goes on vacation to Bali. Do you think she loves him in this situation? Do you think any more evidence is needed that this relationship is not healthy?

She can text him every night, "I miss you. I miss you. It's so boring without you." But she went there for three months, and the guy stayed to work in his town. This girl doesn't love him. This is just one example, of which there are hundreds and thousands.

If you feel that the girl doesn't value the relationship. If you feel that in choosing between some things, she is guided by her selfishness and her current desires. And puts you and your feelings in second position, then she doesn't love you. You don't need her.

One last point. Many girls, in a relationship, are willing to accept everything, and you get nothing in return.

You give her gifts. You give her attention and care. You solve her problems. This kind of relationship is right and normal in a healthy relationship. Both in friendship and in family relationships. You are together to help each other and in that kind of relationship, there is always a payoff. It's not going to be that when she's sick, you don't leave her bedside and make sure she gets better faster. You do everything for that. And when you're sick, she's gone. She's got a lot to do. A lot of work. She was just checking up on you to see how you were feeling. Or she stopped by your house for half an hour and made you tea. And that's it.

A simple example. A girl acts indifferent when you want attention, too. You, like a normal, healthy person (albeit a man) want to be made nice. To give you a gift. To show attention. To think of a way to cheer you up.

When she gives you a gift irresponsibly, buying it on the day of the immediate holiday. She buys the first thing in the store that you don't need and it's okay for her. Then it's not a healthy relationship. She doesn't love you.

But when you, give a gift. You have to make almost every dream come true. She will hint at it and tell you. And if, God forbid, you're wrong about something, she will be angry. You haven't shown proper consideration for her. You haven't been able to understand and figure out what she really wanted. And it's none of her business, she's a woman. It's not that she's a woman. It's that she doesn't love you.

If she doesn't love you, why should she try. But most importantly, she doesn't want you to be happy. And if she doesn't want you to be happy, then she doesn't care about you. She doesn't love you.

If your relationship has been going on for months, you don't need any additional reason to realize that this is the way to the abyss. End that relationship. Take the initiative and go in the direction of the girl who will appreciate you. Keep looking until you find that girl who will love you as much as you will love her.

Don't forget, whoever told you that it doesn't matter to a man whether he is loved or not, it's not true.

For you to love, and be loved, as much as possible.

HOW DO I CONFESS MY FEELINGS? HOW TO TELL A GIRL THAT YOU LOVE HER?

Most men agonize over this question. A guy starts a relationship. Everything is good and everything is going well. For the first few weeks he sees the girl, kisses, cuddles, has sex, and he is incontinent. He absolutely wants to say, "I love you." Without that, he's not comfortable. He doesn't sleep at night, he gets anxious. And there are a lot of guys like that.

It would seem that girls are more emotional and subject to emotions, feelings. No. The situation now is such that a much higher percentage of men can't resist saying "I love you."

If you, don't have a relationship with a girl (you and the girl can't get to some stage), and you want to write that you love her, don't do it. For example, you go on dates with a girl, but she keeps you in a friendzone, you DO NOT have to confess your love for her. No one needs that confession. It will play against you.

For example, you're already kissing, having sex and you're doing fine, everything is great. I would recommend you not to think about confessing your love in the coming months. Let the girl be the first to declare her love to you.

There is a rule of thumb: "He who slows down a relationship, controls it." I advise you to think about this phrase. It's very simple, but very capacious. And it's very helpful to keep in mind about it. Whoever moves more slowly in a relationship is more loved.

If you're speeding up in a relationship that's stuck at some point, you don't have to say "I love you" for the relationship to start moving forward. If you say, "I love you," at that moment, you're not slowing down the relationship, you're trying to speed it up, and you're putting the lever in the girl's hands. She feels that at this point, the balance of importance has shifted to her side. She's more important to you, and she's more desirable to you. This plays against you. Even if she was starting to have feelings for you, that can disappear. So, you don't have to declare your love first. Let the girl, confess first.

"He who slows down a relationship, controls it." It is desirable that this phrase, very seriously rooted in your head. You can write it on a piece of paper or tattoo it on your forehead.

When you're in a relationship and you've been dating for a while. You date for a week, a month, maybe a couple months and she confesses her love to you. She tells you, "I love you." And then guys have the other extreme. They don't say, "I love you." If you're still going to see her, if you want to keep seeing her, then tell her that back. Tell her that you love her too. That's more advantageous for you in this situation, whichever way you look at it. In a situation like this, it's better to respond in the same way than to be stupid and say "thank you." Say what she wants to hear. Even if suddenly, a few weeks or a month later, you realize she's not your option. You'll deal with problems as they come up.

This relationship can end, or it can work out well. And maybe, in fact, things will only get better for you every day.

So, confess your feelings to your girlfriend only when she confesses before. You do not need to do it first.

If you, have this desire, and you do not know who to tell it to, where to stick it, then there is something wrong with you. Rethink everything and realize that it's totally okay to feel and develop a story with a girl without having to say the phrase. And without it, everything will be fine.

HOW TO MAKE A GIRL THINK ABOUT YOU AND MISS YOU?

First, let's understand why this topic is important at all. Why would you want a girl to think about you? Why would you want her to miss you?

The whole point is that when a person falls in love with someone, he begins to think constantly about the object of his crush. Wants to spend as much time as possible with them.

This also works the other way around. If, all of a sudden, a girl will be thinking about some guy all the time. If she will miss him. If she wants to spend as much time with him as possible. She will start to fall in love with him. When a girl is in love with you, then it's up to you to decide what to do with it.

My goal is for the girl to think about you. For her to miss you. How do you do that? The two words that are most important to you are "unique emotions." You need to give a girl an emotion that only you can give her. She can't get that kind of emotion from talking to her girlfriends, from her mom or her co-workers. Or she can't take those emotions from other guys who are hanging around her and asking her out, writing on Instagram and so on. And once you start giving her that kind of emotion, she'll start reaching out to you. I, this is what I call the "drug dealer effect."

A drug dealer, when he gives one or more doses to his new client, he gets him hooked on his product. So you, too, have to give a girl an emotion. You gave it to her once. Another time. And then, she wakes up and she's missing something. At first, she will not understand what it is that she is missing. And then, she'll start reaching out to you. She'll try to communicate with you and she'll want to see you. And that's what we need.

Emotions are unique. What's that about? How does the average man behave? How do 99 out of 100 men behave? They come on a date with a girl and start getting smart and sitting there with a "sour face." They talk about what they do for a living, how they travel, and so on. Tales, maybe, and adequate and maybe even pauses do not arise. But this is impossible to surprise. If a girl goes on ten dates, then almost every guy will behave this way.

But you come on the date. A guy who knows how to flirt. Isn't afraid to use ambiguity and turn conversations into emotional conversations. For example, having conversations about sex in a way that seems natural. So that it looks harmonious and adequate. And in those moments, a girl starts to realize that it's very rare. Maybe she hasn't had one in her life, or has had one for a long time. After such a date, she will talk to her girlfriends, and tell them how great you are. She will, text you between the first and second dates. And out of every one of those interactions, where you laugh, where you talk about cool topics, she'll get used to you. And the code will keep you busy with your hobbies. When you have meetings with friends or busyness at work, she'll start coming in contact with you on her own. Because, she will miss you. Because there's nowhere else she can take that kind of emotion but you.

How do men behave on dates? They come in and talk about their lives like an open book. They lay everything out. They tell you how they spend their time, what they had, how it was, and what their plans are for the coming week.

You don't have to be like an open book. Always leave some mystery. But you don't have to turn into a jerk who hides absolutely everything. Who you work with, your hobbies, and so on. Play the mystery guy.

Sometimes when she asks: "How was your day?" All you have to do is answer, "I had a lot to do." And she'll embellish herself and make up her own mind and fantasize somewhere. So if you wanted to promote yourself and you failed, don't tell her your schedule by the minute. Sometimes that's what guys do. So, leave moments for her to look at you as a mystery. This will be very helpful.

As a rule, most guys, have very low self-esteem. And this manifests itself in the fact that they swamp the girl with a huge amount of flattery and compliments. Instead of teasing at some moments or in a playful and joking way, in a good way, to make fun of her.

When you start talking about yourself, don't spill your complexes on the table. Don't think that with such sincerity or maybe pity, you'll be able to get her to like you. Love yourself, start working on your self-esteem. Because if you love yourself, if you appreciate yourself, this will be transmitted to the girl. She will treat you, just like you treat yourself.

A very important point about how you should behave with girls. You have to be a little bit lacking. You don't have to be like "gooey candy." Don't be the one who tries to completely fill up all his time talking to her.

How does a guy act when he goes on a date? He sits around waiting for her to write. As soon as she writes, he instantly writes back. It seems like a small thing, but it's not the right thing to do. As soon as she hints that she's ready to meet, he immediately drives across town to her place. That's not a good thing to do. It seems petty. And it may not seem like a big deal to you, but that's how 99 out of 100 guys act. You have to behave differently. Give unique emotions. Be unique.

Try to end the date yourself. Or try to interrupt the correspondence at the most interesting point. For example, she wrote you something interesting, and you reply the next day. Say you were distracted and had a lot to do. And I hope that you are adequate. I hope you won't do it all in one hour.

These days, girls are in great short supply, from guys who know their worth. Who don't turn into fanatics for that girl after the first date. So, keep a balance.

Try, challenge yourself. Finish the date first. Tell her, "Cool chatting, everything's super, but I have to go, I have things to do."

If you agreed to meet, then reschedule it yourself. And say, "Look, I'm sorry, but I can't see you today. Let's do it next time." Or don't answer her message or don't answer her messages for a long time. And that's enough.

If the girl is beautiful, she's not used to this kind of

communication. Because, she has a herd of suitors, who at any moment, at the first call, are ready to hang around her.

The next point, which is very important. Work on the richness of your life. The more interesting things happen in your life, the more she will be drawn to you. You will be (in a good way) different from most men. Because, with most men, it's talk about work and dating. All of these conversations, the girl knows perfectly well. And as soon as, she bumps into a guy with a lot of interests and a lot of passion for some things, it gives her a new unfamiliar emotion. She'll reach out to you more.

Don't forget that the more, you're not like all the standard, dumb-ass guys she usually goes out with. The more likely she is to get more hooked on you and think about you. She'll start to miss you and fall in love with you accordingly.

Work on yourself. Work on your self-esteem. Work on the fact that you can give girls a completely different range of emotions. And in a favorable light, different from most guys today. A large part of modern society.

HOW DO YOU GET A GIRL TO RUN FOR YOU?

In my mind, this is something abnormal. In this desire, in this question, as a woman who makes a man a henpecked. There is no happiness in such a relationship. It's concerning when a girl starts running after you.

Guys who are very serious about the goal: How do you get a girl to run after them? They usually don't succeed. But there are men who, very often, do have it happen that women start running after them. They show a lot of (even excessive) attention. They are ready, for various feats, just to see this man.

I would like to highlight the main points. Why does it happen in some people's lives that women run after them, fall in love with them, but for others, it's quite bad.

Guys and men that women run after. What's so special about them?

Number one. It's the value of the relationship. How they feel about relationships. You've probably heard a woman say, "If you don't like it, leave." Very often this happens in the initial stages. When on a date, a guy tries to open his mouth and say that he does not like something about the girl. Then very often, you can hear: "If you don't like it, leave." This is something to take for granted.

Guys that girls are very strongly attracted to (especially in the initial stages of a relationship) have such a value of a relationship that this value, is zero.

A guy is willing to accept absolutely anything. If it's going to be the last time he meets her, it's not a problem for him. He's not thinking ten meetings in advance. He's not making any romantic illusions or plans with this girl. He lives for one moment. If this meeting is the last one for him, he won't be upset. It's helpful when you have that attitude (especially in the early stages) as well.

You're like a man who works hard and strives for something. Has the right to just come home after work, lie down on the couch and relax. Do nothing, watch a series and drink a beer. But only the girls you hang out with don't need to know about it. It's in your own interest to create the illusion that you're always busy.

There are guys who go to the gym after work. Have lots of meetings with friends and so on. Their lives are boiling. But if, that's not the case with you. You come home after work, you start texting with her. You're in touch with her 24/7. And as soon as, she needs something, there you are. As soon as she texts, you answer right away. You're like an open book in front of her. So she's not interested in you. This is one of the elements of mystery, which is necessary if you want a girl to run after you.

Make her think about what you're doing there. What's going on in your life? Not like she knows your daily routine completely. What you do and what you eat. That kind of information, in the early stages, is a very serious hindrance to you. Even if you don't realize it.

Next point. I call it unpredictability. You could also call it "the spectrum of emotions.

I have an acquaintance who gets a lot of attention from girls. And in terms of logic. After another one of his antics. The girl should not pick up the phone at all, not answer and not want to spend much time with him. Why? Because, he's such a creative person, and he can disappear at some point. For five to seven days, turn off his phone and don't go on social media. It's impossible to get in contact with him. How does that work for a girl? At a meeting, he says nice words to her, gives her emotions, and then disappears. She tries to contact him. For a few days, she looks for him. He gets in touch like nothing ever happened. He says he misses her and suggests we meet. In response to her tantrums and emotions, he calmly says, as if that's the way it should be: "I was busy and just got free. When I got free, I called you right away." That's a unique emotion. It's a unique emotion that she, can't find an approach to. And a lot of people are blown away by that. There are girls who don't fall for this kind of manipulation. But those who are hooked on this hook get hooked on it. Even if the guy starts talking nonsense.

To get a girl to chase you. You have to have cosmic self-love. Self-confidence. Love for yourself and the understanding that you're a really cool guy who has something to love. To the question, why isn't she falling in love with me? Why doesn't she run after me? A self-confident man, won't ask such questions.

We all know very well that girls love themselves much more. They are much more used to the framework they have. Either you fit into that frame or you go away. Men tend to start, question their limits.

So, you have to be confident in yourself. Your thoughts, have a very serious effect on those around you. It has a very serious effect on women. And when a woman encounters a man who has boundless self-love, it affects her as well. She also begins to penetrate to you, more strong feelings, strong emotions. This leads to the fact that she starts to want you. She starts to look for a meeting with you and impose herself. She will ask for your attention and emotions. This is exactly the picture we get when we say a girl is chasing a guy. Try to use what you read to your advantage.

WHAT TO DO IF A GIRL IGNORES YOU?

Doesn't answer your calls, messages, but you wait, hope and believe.

First you have to start with the question: Why has she started ignoring you? This is very important. Sometimes, it's enough to answer the question: What to do? And do it. But in this particular case, if you don't know the reason. If you don't know why? You're not going to take seriously the recommendation, what to do?

So, take a couple of minutes on this issue. I would break down the situation of being ignored by the girl into two separate options.

First. She started ignoring you when your story didn't even begin. I have an example of this.

A successful, well-formed man, a businessman. I went up to a girl in a nightclub to get acquainted. She said she wouldn't introduce herself. He, found her on Facebook, texted her: "Hi. Let's meet tonight." But she didn't respond. He thinks she's trying to get her price that way. So he, begins to be persistent.

In his mind, the reason - why? Totally unformed and misguided.

If your story hasn't even begun. If you only wrote " Hello" to a girl you liked on Instagram or Facebook or whatever, and she doesn't respond to your messages. This means that from the beginning, she wasn't interested in you. I'll put it in simple terms. I hope this doesn't offend you too much. She didn't like you. And that's okay. Because absolutely everyone only likes a $100 bill. Neither you or I are a $100 bill. So, some people may like us, and some people may not like us. That's okay. The sooner you realize that, the better off you'll be.

If at the start, when there was not even communication with the girl, there were no dates, no correspondence, there was nothing between you. And the girl ignores and doesn't respond to you in any way, the story is over. Forget about her and move on to the next girl. You don't have to do anything. To the question, what to do? Do nothing in this situation. Accept it. Treat it like an adult with an understanding man, not a romantic with a romantic outlook on life.

Maybe your mother or your kindergarten teacher told you that a girl should be pursued. "Find out where she works. Find out where she lives and send flowers. Write 10 messages." That's not going to work. You'll only waste your energy, and your time. So, in this case, don't do anything.

There is another situation. When some process went on, and you've been texting for a long time. Or you've even had a date. And at some point, the girl stops contacting you. At that point, she stops responding to your messages. Doesn't respond to an offer to meet. Things haven't gone according to the plan you had in mind. In this case, there is a reason. A very rare reason is that the girl is offended. More often than not, the reason is that from your interaction with her, you didn't meet her expectations. You didn't interest her. In such cases, the problem is not the first impression of you, but directly your actions.

Your communication was from the bottom up. You, as the "the accessible man," were blocking her from breathing in the here and now. You texted her often and showed her several times a day that you were constantly available. "And how was your day? What did you eat? I'm ready to see you whenever you want." At this point, you weren't acting like "candy." You weren't sweet, you were sticky. That's a big problem with men.

Just when a guy has met a girl, he's already laying his life completely on her altar. He starts, thanking her after every date. He floods her with compliments. He lies down at her feet. From such, a normal girl begins to be repulsed. You don't want to hang out with men like that.

The second problem that comes up a lot. It's when she gives you the opportunity to express yourself. For example: the first date and you just talk to her. Second date, and you're just talking to her. You don't try to kiss her. You have no desire to have sex with

CHAPTER 4: IT CAN'T BE IGNORED IN A RELATIONSHIP

8 Things You Can't Forgiven A Woman

Men were asked the question, "After what, would you be willing to end the relationship?" 98 percent of men always state that after cheating. "If she cheats on me, there will be no continuation of the relationship. Cheating is unacceptable to me." Seems like a reason to be proud. 98 percent of men have self-esteem and self-respect. They have some kind of rules, criteria for relationships. It seems cool, but the reality is much tougher. 98 percent of men say they're ready to end a relationship. In practice, when they find out that a woman has cheated on them, not every one of them ends the relationship.

Unfortunately, a lot of men, live in this reality that if a woman has cheated, then there is a reason and you have to understand this reason, and fix it in yourself. And when you fix those issues, then you can continue to build a relationship with her and you'll be fine, you'll live happily ever after.

If you've had cheating in your relationship, if your woman has cheated on you, end the relationship, dump her.

Those 98 percent of men who were asked this question also asked, "What else does a girl have to do to get you to break up with her?" And one in two, can't find anything else to say. About the cheating, they know, they've heard, and the rest is no big deal. "I'm going to hold on to this relationship, fight," and so on.

You learn 7 more things to do, after which you can be sure the relationship needs to end. On a foundation like that, no happy continuation, can happen.

The second act I want to talk about is when a girl goes missing for a few days. And this happens a lot. More often than not, it happens in a relationship when you're not living together.

In the relationship stage, when you haven't moved in together yet. It happens that a girl can disappear for a few days or a day, even if you live together. Went to her friend's house and doesn't pick up the phone. In the evening does not pick up, tomorrow does not pick up, and only some time later she calls and says: "I was talking to my friend and tired, so I could not answer. Now my love, I'm on my way home." For example, she might say she's on her way to her parents' house and forgot her phone. And you're worried that something might have happened to her. Think about how she sees this relationship, what's the value of you if she hasn't even thought of you these days. If suddenly, your girlfriend is gone (let's not go to extremes, and subtract minutes) for more than one day, this relationship needs to end. You don't need to hear that she was really tired, forgot, or someone distracted her, had a headache, and so on. Fuck it all. If she's gone for more than a day, and she hasn't responded to your texts, hasn't picked up the phone, end the relationship.

Third reason. She accepts gifts.

Some, even proud when his girlfriend, other guys, give gifts and flowers. Think about this girl's values. You are in a triangle. At this point, you are a higher priority for her, but by accepting gifts, she is already giving him hope. Slowly developing a story with him. Is it necessary to be in this kind of relationship? Do you need to be okay with it? Shouldn't you consider that when your girlfriend, who is in a relationship with you, is given a gift by someone and she accepts it. That tells you that she's mercurial. She doesn't appreciate or love you. So if, all of a sudden, your girlfriend accepts gifts, other men, fuck her.

The fourth act, she doesn't accept your rules.

When you and your girlfriend start dating, you're having a great time, eating, drinking, having sex and at some point, your story spills over into a sultry relationship. And when that happens, you spell out some rules. In some cases, it's directly spelled out, and in some cases, it's just a consequence when you're communicating with a girl. You communicate and you see a different picture of each other's lives. You see the rules of life, and you label those rules. For example, you can't communicate with exes. For example, "we're already in a relationship, but I'm not comfortable with you going out with some of your guy friends." It's one thing when she was a single girl and went to nightclubs with her friends. It's another thing for her to be in a relationship with you. When you negotiate the rules, it could be that your relationship history will end in the beginning, that's totally fine. A relationship, it's not a cage or a penal colony where you're forced to do something.

If she accepted your rules, and then it turns out that she didn't in the relationship.

For example, she heard you and she will not communicate with her ex, and then it turns out that she is communicating with him. She promised you no more nightclubs, but when she says she's going to her mom's, you find out she went to a club. With that, she throws in the trash, the rules you negotiated. The rules on which your relationship with her was formed. They weren't formed on the fact that you can have sex and eat together. So if she doesn't accept the outlined rules, that relationship needs to end.

Next step. The girl says to you, "We need to break up." No matter what situation this happened. In an argument, when she's drunk and you hear the phrase: "We have to break up," the relationship has to end. You shouldn't be misled if she says "maybe we should break up" or "perhaps we should break up" on every occasion, no, that's the same thing. In whatever situation or with whatever intonation you hear that she's ready to end the relationship, you have to take matters into your own hands. You need to make the decision yourself and end the relationship, and never communicate with her again after that.

Another phrase you might hear is: "We need to take a pause" and "I need to sort myself out." There is no pause. There's just the fact that right now she doesn't love you, and she doesn't appreciate you. She wants to try some new story and start dating someone else. If things don't work out better with him, she'll settle for you and try to get back with you. You don't need that. I hope you have enough self-respect. Your goal is to be a happy man, so you don't have to settle for that kind of relationship. So if you hear from a girl that she wants to "take a break from the relationship," the relationship needs to end, or rather it is already over. Have the courage to admit it. Have the courage and determination to end it completely and forever. If a girl says, "I need to sort myself out," that's just a pretty phrase. With that she's saying, "I'm not happy with you, I don't like what's going on between us enough. I think I deserve more and better." She'll see if she can make it with someone else, and you wait, or better yet, "Dance around me and show me how much you need me, maybe I'll agree to it." Only, if she does agree, expect her to make another run at you about how she "needs to sort herself out." To you, that's an indicator that a happy relationship isn't going to happen. It won't.

Next act. The girl insults you. This includes insulting your friends that you love. Relatives you love. Even if, for example, your parents are problematic and not right or perfect. But it's one thing when you yourself say something bad about them, it's another thing when your girlfriend starts to talk about them and they haven't done anything bad to her.

In very many relationships, and very often there is a situation where a girl starts to call her boyfriend bad names. Starts talking badly about his appearance, insults his hobbies, tries to mock his successes. You come in feeling elated, start talking about what's going on in your life, and she tries to make fun of you, tries to humiliate you. She might tell you to fuck off. Or sitting at the same table with you, saying nasty things. Any insult to you, that's the end of the relationship. If you see a girl insulting you, mocking you, your lifestyle, end that relationship. It's like a snowball, it's only going to get bigger and bigger and bigger. It will never stop. If you think you're going to suck it up now and she's going to realize what a great, good guy you are and it's going to stop, no. It's going to get bigger and bigger.

And the last act, it's various manipulations. It's more like a collective image, too. She's constantly talking about how she doesn't feel like a girl, that she likes this and she doesn't like that, acting this way is good and acting that way is bad. This kind of manipulation by a certain kind of woman, sooner or later manifests itself so much that not a day goes by without her "blowing your mind" with her tears, tantrums and scandals. It becomes your reality. All of this is the stuff of your relationship. Therefore, manipulation in any form is terrible. If you see manipulation by your woman, end the relationship.

SIGNS IN A RELATIONSHIP THAT SHOULD NOT BE IGNORED

As soon as a man gets excited, as soon as he sees a beautiful girl in front of him (even during a large number of meetings), he forgets about logic. He forgets to notice and pay attention to how she behaves and doesn't draw conclusions from it. He begins to build a relationship with a girl who is totally wrong for him.

What kind of things do girls do and what kind of signs should you pay attention to?

If you want to be in a relationship with a girl who is worthy of it and suitable for the relationship. The first thing you need to pay attention to is her friends. Especially if she spends a lot of time with them. If you understand that each of her friends is cheating on her boyfriend. Each of her girlfriends is completely unserious about the relationship she is in. (After all, it's a weird way of life when she's not committed to anything). Your girlfriend, then, will be just like them. She is the one who chose these girlfriends.

There is an expression, "Friends, are the family we can choose." The girl chooses these friends. There's a reason for that. Even if you haven't noticed some qualities in her yet, anyway, she has those qualities, which are present in her friends. So if her friends are a "ball of snakes" then this girl is not suitable for you.

Second point. Signs of anger and disrespectful attitude towards others. What is this about?

When she's interacting with you, she's all sweet, she's kind, she's smiling and she's just wonderful. But, when the waiter comes up who, interrupts her when she was telling you something or he makes a mistake. She ordered sparkling water and he brought non-carbonated water. She starts talking to him in a completely different way than she does to you. Or when her mother calls her, she starts instantly snapping, yelling into the phone, acting inappropriately and inadequately.

It doesn't seem to matter to you. Because, with you, she's smiling. She touches your hand and wishes you a nice appetite when you're sitting in a restaurant eating something. She acts normal with you. You feel like that's the way it should be. The main thing is that to you, she treats you well. But the thing is, in front of you, she is trying to show herself in the right light. She's trying to impress you.

But, there will come a point when she thinks that she doesn't need to give the impression of a "good girl" in front of you anymore either. She doesn't need to play a role. Then, she'll start acting just like she does with the waiter, the cab driver, her mom. Or maybe her old girlfriend.

Pay attention to this and in a few meetings, you will clearly begin to notice the difference in the girl's behavior with you and with those around her. If the difference is catastrophic. When you see that she changes in her facial expression, in her tone of voice, in her emotions, it's a very bad sign. It's a terrible sign. That girl is definitely not right for you.

Next point. The girl thinks it's okay not to be invested in the relationship.

Talk about the beginning of a relationship. Maybe you've already been on five dates or six, seven, eight. Maybe you've already had sex with her and some of your meetings are at your house. If those meetings are getting bigger and bigger, and the girl never once bothers to grab something to eat. Or she knows you work a lot, and she says, "You said you liked pancakes with meat. I'll make them this weekend, and I'll bring them to you tomorrow." If there's no show of caring on her part. She doesn't care about you. If she has absolutely no desire to do anything to make this relationship go forward. You don't need a girl like that.

For example, you don't offer to see her for two days and she doesn't say, "I missed you and am waiting for us to meet. You need to understand that it's not going to be that as soon as you give her some jewelry or a ring, her behavior will change toward you. No. You're facing a person who isn't going to, and won't under any circumstances, do anything to make you happy in the relationship either. The only person she cares about her happiness is herself and you don't need a girl like that.

Next, a very important point. There are some people who make fun of absolutely everything. Sarcasm, when it is served in moderation and at the right time, is a good thing. But there are people who try to hide a huge number of complexes that they have.

Everything is wrong for her. She tries to comment on everything: the waiter's clothes, the way you hold your fork and knife, the way you stir the sugar, the music, the interior, the way people talk, and so on. She dislikes absolutely everything. All of this, she serves with a kind of mockery and derision and the flow of it doesn't stop. This flow goes on and on. In this way, she is not trying to demonstrate that she is a cheerful girl with a good sense of humor. She's trying to hide her complexes, which will very soon weigh you down. You don't want a girl who acts like that. Don't take a girl like that for a serious relationship.

The girl uses the expression, "All men are assholes."

She does this while talking about her past relationships. She had all the wrong guys. One man hit, another man drank, another man stole, and she was soft and fluffy. In some men, there is a desire to protect, to warm. "Why is life unfair. Why does such a good and wonderful girl only get jerks. I have to be a hero to her. I have to turn her life into a fairy tale."

She chose these men and was with them for a while. She knew they weren't nice. But when, they became her exes, it's much easier for her to call them names than to find the problem in herself. It's much easier for her to speak negatively about them than to try to sort things out and find fault with herself. She doesn't try to correct her behavior. So if a girl, on a date, starts to throw mud all over her past relationships. Know that you're facing the kind of girl who is very quick, with any of her problems, to say that you're a asshole. She'll say you're an idiot. She'll say it in front of everyone: her girlfriends, her parents. In front of everyone around her. She'll talk trash about you. A person who is not capable of admitting his mistakes is not suitable for a serious relationship.

WHY DO WOMEN CHEAT?

If a partner is looking for a reason to cheat, they will find one.

The main reason women cheat, and the only reason they cheat, they want to cheat. They believe that cheating, it is absolutely normal. These women, thought so before the relationship with you, during the relationship with you, when they haven't cheated yet, but want it madly and are looking for a reason to do it. If a girl is a slut inside, it's not going anywhere. She will cheat on you over and over again. She will cheat in subsequent relationships.

There are problems in relationships. Problems come big, problems come small, and you can't get away from it. These problems can cause a relationship to end. Some people, get this problem solved by a mutual effort, or someone for two tries to solve the problem. But there are times when the problem is not solved and this problem can be the reason for the relationship to end. This does not justify a person being an idiot and cheating. If a girl, inside, has, "I want to cheat. I'm ready to cheat. I will cheat," she will find a reason that will allow her to not think she is guilty and think she is fine and it is the man's fault.

If you find out that a girl has cheated in a past relationship, (she can tell you 80 reasons why she cheated in a past relationship) you can be sure that in your relationship with you too, she will find a reason why it is okay for her to cheat on you too. When in your relationship, the woman cheated on you, she will say you are the reason. She'll find one, two or three reasons why she had to cheat on you. And she's so great, she's just an angel, you're the one who forced her to cheat. She'll say you have to change, and she won't cheat on you. Rest assured, she will cheat on you. It's a part of her, it's a part that's not going anywhere. So if you're trying to figure it out and find a reason why your woman cheated on you, know the reason is, just one, she's a slut.

CHEATING! HOW TO KNOW IF A GIRLS IS CHEATING ON YOU?

We dream of the perfect relationship, but it's bad when that relationship ends in nothing. It's even worse if that relationship cheats on you and the other half cheats on you. Much worse if it goes on for a long time and you are in complete ignorance.

Signs that your girlfriend is cheating on you.

In fact, any person is much stupider than he would like or than he thinks. Signs that a loved one is cheating, have, absolutely everyone. The most important thing is not to put on the rose-coloured glasses. Do not close your eyes to the signs that you notice, and make the right conclusions.

The first sign that your girlfriend is cheating on you. She's constantly texting with someone.

She comes home from work and is texting with someone. You go out, she's constantly texting with someone. She picks up her phone even when she goes to the bathroom. The sympathy, for some lover of hers is so great that she puts it on the scale, to be caught in front of you or to respond to him in time. She chooses him. The main thing is not to turn a blind eye to it. The main thing is not to believe her. You ask, "Who are you texting there? and you're smiling." She replies: "A work friend." If that happens, it's a sign that she's cheating on you.

The second sign that a girl is cheating on you is a change in behavior toward you.

It so happens that people after cheating start to feel internal discomfort. For example, men, very often, after cheating start to shower their wives with gifts, flowers and so on. For girls, most of the time the opposite is true. Girls after adultery, begin to show aggression towards his boyfriend. She starts to get pissed off that you're smacking or you put your socks in the wrong place after you come home from work. You're starting to piss her off about some little things that before, she didn't even pay attention to.

But now there are girls who, on the contrary, try to make up for it. Pay more attention. They start sending a lot more hearts, kisses. She tells you how important you are to her and so on. Although before, there was nothing like that on her part, not even close.

This also applies to changes in terms of sex. Some girls, after cheating, cut you off completely access to your body. And some, start pestering you several times more and demand sex from you even more than she demanded before. Pay attention to this, by all means.

The third sign that your girlfriend is cheating on you is a change in her schedule.

Suddenly, constant delays at work until late at night have begun. She's loaded up on extra work. The girlfriend has to help with the baby or move some things. Therefore, she suddenly (which you didn't notice before) started coming home from work, much later.

She began to often ask how you are? How are your plans? What time will you be back from the gym today? If you're going out with friends, approximately what time you'll be back? Aren't you going to be early. At first, this behavior, you'll think you're caring and attentive on her part, but really, you have to be very, very careful about such moments.

Also pay attention to the way she behaves with you in phone conversations. She might call you and say, "I wanted to tell you that we're having a company party at work. I probably won't be in touch for the next hour or two. So, I thought I'd call you and give you a heads up." Very often, this kind of call is made to show you that you just talked and for a while, you won't bother her. And she, won't be caught while she's with her lover.

One of the important things about schedules and phone conversations. If, very often, during her delays at work, when you call her to find out when she will be back, there is no signal or no answer. This is a sign that she has been cheating on you for a long time.

A fourth sign that your girlfriend is cheating on you is a change in her appearance.

She's started caring a lot more about how she looks. It's not done for you, not during meetings when you go out for a walk or go visiting. It's done before she leaves the house. She has started going to work and is always wearing a lot of makeup. She's constantly dressing in a way that tries to increase her sexuality. This is not done for you. Notice that if she, all of a sudden, is paying a lot more attention to her appearance when she leaves the house, it means that there is someone to show it to. There's someone to try for. And since, it's not done during your time together and not for you, think about who? Most likely for the guy she's already cheating on you with.

The fifth sign is to pay attention to your intuition. This is a very important feeling, which, in no case, can not be ignored. One way or another, you are already in a long relationship with this girl. You notice something about her, and it's quite possible that what you notice doesn't add up to any logical chain. You see that there's a change. You realize that something is changing, and changing, not in favor of your relationship. Take a closer look. If your intuition tells you that you are being cheated on, you really are being cheated on.

FEMALE MANIPULATION IN RELATIONSHIPS "YOU DON'T TRUST ME?"

Let's talk about female manipulation. Specifically, the manipulation of the phrase: "You don't trust me?

As a rule, in the most serious and insidious situations, you can hear this phrase. If in your relationship, there was something like this, then you need to be very careful.

For example, your girlfriend or wife returns from work and says: "My friend from the neighboring department found a good trip to the sea. She offers to fly with her, to relax. Will you let me go?". You think, "Wow, even asks permission," but you realize that this idea is stupid. You realize it's utter nonsense and in a relationship, it's unacceptable. You say, "No." She says, "Don't you trust me? Do you really think that once I'm under the scorching sun, have a couple of cocktails, I won't be able to control myself? Can't control myself? You disappoint me. That's insulting to me. You don't trust me? You have to trust me."

Or another example. She decides to go out for coffee with some friend of hers (who you recently found out about). You resent it, but she lights up, "I treat him just like a friend. What kind of suspicion is that on your part?" Or you notice her texting and you ask her, "Who are you texting with?" to which she replies: "With a friend." You realize this is repeating itself, time after time, and it looks kind of weird. You ask her to show you, but the answer you get is, "You don't trust me? You have no idea how much you've insulted me."

It's manipulative in that any act is replaced by your guilt. You stop thinking about what she is doing. She starts acting inappropriately. She starts to make you think there's something wrong with you. That you have some complexes and unfounded suspicions. All of this, turns into a scheme, and the girl goes to the sea, and you also blame yourself throughout her trip. And when she comes back, you ask her to forgive you for not trusting her. That you are so bad. That you're going to work on yourself. That you're ruining her life. That you're making this relationship toxic. At that point, she's a winner and you're an absolute loser.

A very important point, as with any manipulation. You have to understand, what is this manipulation? And how do you fight it? It's very easy to fight it. Regardless of whether you trust it or not. Regardless of how the people around you, your parents, her parents and so on, will look at this act. It doesn't matter if this act is good or not, if it has a place in the relationship or not. If a girl wants to go on vacation to the sea or any other country without you. If she is going to do it without you, this girl is doing things that are not allowed in a normal relationship.

If the girl wants to go to a meeting, have coffee or something more with some obscure friend of hers: this, she is doing things that are unacceptable in your relationship. A normal man who loves his partner, a normal girl who loves her man, she will not do that. A normal man who loves his girlfriend, he won't do that. You don't have to explain it to her. You don't need to look at it through the prism of "trust, don't trust". The person will not do that.

You can tell her, "It's not about trust. It's about why, in your head, is this kind of thing considered normal? I'm not going on vacation with my friends without you. I'd rather go with you or take you with me. I'm not going to go to a meeting with some friend of mine and have coffee. I'm not going to go to a club with my friends. I can only go with you or spend the evening with you. I'm doing all the things that emphasize that I value our relationship to me. A girl who is in a relationship with me won't do that. I don't want a girl who wants to vacation without me. I don't want a girl who goes to meetings with some obscure friends."

Don't forget that in any manipulation, you have to be ready to go all the way. After all, you, don't want a girl who is ready to do things like that.

FEMALE MANIPULATION "WE NEED TO BREAK UP!"

Another type of feminine manipulation: "We need to break up." This is an attempt to test a guy to see if he is ready to end the relationship.

This test happens when the relationship is in its initial phase. The girl, at some point (when nothing seems to portend anything serious), says to the guy: "We need to break up." Usually, this comes via text message or social media. Much less often, it happens in person. Nevertheless, these situations do happen.

Even now, I remember the story of one of my acquaintances. He had been dating a girl for a few months. This guy approached the relationship thoroughly. He arranged all sorts of surprises for his girlfriend. He was constantly trying to diversify their relationship. It was not a typical relationship. It was almost impossible to accuse the guy of not investing enough in the relationship. But at one point, the girl said to him, "You know, I'm bored with this relationship. We need to break up."

If you hear from a girl, a suggestion that: "We need to break up," instantly take the initiative into your own hands. Say, "You know, I really think (especially if you suggest it yourself), it's better this way." This happens when you meet her in person. If a girl writes this to you in a message, social media, you don't have to respond to it. This is one example of when the technique, "closer - farther" is applied. This is when you have to respond to a girl's "farther," with your deeper "farther." If she ignores you, you have to respond to her with the same action.

Typically, this manipulation, happens in the relatively initial stages. When you've been dating for a month. Not every offer to break up is manipulation. It's entirely possible that you've made mistakes in the relationship. It's entirely possible that something didn't work out for you, so the relationship ends.

But very often, a girl doesn't really want the relationship to end. She wants, in this way, to train you. If she says she's ready to end the relationship: you'll start convincing her, showering her with gifts and "beating your chest" and saying whatever it takes to keep the relationship going. By these actions, you're getting one step closer to becoming a henpecked. The girl "bends" you to her will. You can't be guided by self-respect, and you start fawning over her. This is just the first step.

Also, such manipulation, can be a test. How truly worthy a man is in front of her. Who does not pass this test, then in the eyes of the girl, his value goes down.

So as not to succumb, to this type of manipulation. If you still want a relationship with a girl who is trying to manipulate you, you need to know how best to behave.

When the girl says, "We have to break up. Do not try to prove that you madly love her. Don't try to prove that you need this relationship. Don't try to give gifts. You should, on the contrary, ignore her at some point. Reply to her, "If that's the way you want it, let's go on with our lives." You can even, push a little jealousy. Miss out for a while and don't respond to her messages. Get as far away from her as possible. At times like this the opposite reaction will work.

At some point, the girl herself will start checking on you. She'll start texting, asking you something. If you, at this point, keep a cool mind and a sober head, she will start to ask back to you.

It happened to the acquaintance I was talking about. A girl asked him to break up with her. He pulled himself together and agreed. And almost the next day, she immediately said, "You know, I realized everything. I love you. I can't be without you. I've been a fool," and so on. He forgave her. It's hard to say here whether he was right or wrong.

Everyone, in their particular example, will make the decision they think is right. But when a girl offers to break up, support that decision, take the initiative. It will look as if this decision came from you too. Only you're, a second too late to voice it. And everything will be fine. Don't fall for a woman's manipulation.

CONCLUSION

Most guys will drop this book without taking any action to improve their lives. Such people expect that everything they want should come true instantly, but that's not the case. After reading this book or hundreds of others on how to seduce or meet the girl of your dreams, dozens of motivational books won't give you results if you do nothing. Do something and you'll get what you want. Start small. In the beginning, as in any endeavor, there will be failures and unsuccessful results, but there will be no growth without it. Mistakes will help you become better at dating girls.

Start taking your life seriously, because no one else will do it for you. You're the only one responsible for your life.

www.ingramcontent.com/pod-product-compliance
Ingram Content Group UK Ltd.
Pitfield, Milton Keynes, MK11 3LW, UK
UKHW021923190726
13853UKWH00002B/816

9 798846 093485